DISCERNING
Religious Life

DISCERNING
Religious Life

SISTER CLARE MATTHIASS, CFR

VIANNEY VOCATIONS

Vianney Vocations, Valdosta, Georgia
© Sister Clare Matthiass, CFR
All rights reserved. Published 2017
Printed in the United States of America

ISBN: 978-0-9896212-5-0

LCCN: 2017939431

Nihil obstat: Rev. Douglas K. Clark, STL
Imprimatur: Most Rev. Gregory J. Hartmayer, OFM Conv.,
D.D., Bishop of Savannah

Cover design by Darcie Riordan and Sam Alzheimer

A gift for Our Lady

In memory of

Fr. Benedict Groeschel, CFR
† October 3, 2014

Ron Novotny, PhD, STL
† May 31, 2015

Fr. Michael Scanlan, TOR
† January 7, 2017

with profound gratitude and love

Contents

Foreword

"What would the Church be without you?" How clearly I remember the question that Pope Francis asked while thanking the religious sisters of the United States during his visit to St. Patrick's Cathedral in 2015. As he thanked them for their efforts, the congregation broke into spontaneous, sustained applause! Yet we know so well that our beloved sisters are not in religious life for the accolades, for the applause—not at all! They are in it because they have responded to God's call to love and serve Him through the beautiful gift of consecrated life. So I am grateful that Sr. Clare Matthiass, CFR, has provided this thorough, practical guide for women prayerfully discerning a vocation to religious life.

If you have studied American history, you will recall that Catholics often faced great challenges and prejudices as they came to the United States. Yet you might be surprised to learn that one of the most important factors that improved the view that many previously suspicious Americans had of Catholics was the witness of religious sisters during the Civil War. The

sisters were present on the major battlefields during that trag-
ic event, caring for the wounded of both sides, often with little
regard for their own lives. Their heroic care and compassion
convinced many to rethink their prejudices against Catholics.

Why does this matter to a woman discerning a vocation
in the twenty-first century? I propose that this historical example, as well as the witness of so many other great wom-
en religious of the United States—St. Elizabeth Ann Seton, St.
Frances Xavier Cabrini, to name just a few—all demonstrate
the heart of religious life: love and service. Love of God and
neighbor, demonstrated through acts of service, in outreach
to the poor, in education, by evangelizing those who do not
know Jesus. This has always been the driving force of religious life and you will see why in the pages of this book, which
honestly and joyfully addresses those at any stage of the discernment process.

Sister Clare provides valuable guidance to assist wom-
en trying to better understand what a commitment to religious life entails. Many people naturally wonder: "What will
my life be like?" By drawing on the experiences of several
sisters living out their vocation today, you will see the variety of expressions that are possible, as well as the consistent
themes of love and service. I would also point out another key truth that is evident in this work and in the experience of religious sisters everywhere: for one who is discerning, prayer and participation in the sacramental life of the
Church must be central. It is the love of God, made present
to us through His Word and sacraments, that gives us the
grace to say yes to His call, so we must always remain close
to Him as we discern.

The people of God so often tell me about their love and gratitude for the sisters—a love and gratitude I certainly share! I was educated by faithful and dedicated sisters, and have had countless opportunities to see the many ways that communities of religious women are sharing God's love with others. Whether we are talking about the Civil War or the needs of today, we cannot imagine the Church without sisters. I am sure you remember these beautiful words of Pope Francis: "The thing the church needs most today is the ability to heal wounds and to warm the hearts of the faithful; it needs nearness, proximity. I see the church as a field hospital after battle." We know that where there is a field hospital, there will be sisters!

Whether you are just beginning to think about a vocation to religious life or have been wrestling with it for years, you will find great wisdom in this book to assist you. And just as your own prayer life is central to discernment, I assure you that I always keep those women discerning a vocation in my prayers.

Timothy Michael Cardinal Dolan
Archbishop of New York
April 2017

Introduction

I n a city of six million people, where billions of dollars change hands in the course of a normal day, in a city where there are sexual references every few feet, and everybody seems proud to be making their own way and doing their own thing, four beautiful, intelligent women lay prostrate on the cold marble floor of Our Lady of Good Counsel Church and gave their lives entirely to God as they vowed to live lives of poverty, chastity and obedience. It was ten o'clock on a Monday morning in Manhattan. The six hundred people who had taken time off work and packed the beautiful church on 90th Street were just about the only people who knew of the profound, eternal mystery taking place as the city whirled on as usual.

It isn't how many people are aware of an event that gives it its significance. Did anyone at all know what was happening at Joachim and Anne's house when the angel Gabriel and the Blessed Virgin Mary had a conversation that would change everything for everyone for all time? Or the Resurrection of Jesus from the dead? It is difficult to imagine a more significant event in human history, and yet, there was not one person present to witness it. God's actions are His own, accomplished by His design, His initiative, and His power. And so it is with the choosing, the calling, and the consecration of religious women. It is His prerogative, His work, and His will. And the world goes on, with few who notice. "Hidden" is the mode for the divine mysteries.

These four sisters can look forward to a fairly hidden life. They will be known to their sisters and brothers in community,[1] to the homeless who come to the door every day, to the children who come to Upper Room[2] youth group, to the patrons of the Father Solanus Soup Kitchen,[3] and to friends who support the community. They have been, and will be, mistaken for each other, and they have already become accustomed to a certain anonymity that goes along with being a religious sister. They will have neither children nor grandchildren to keep their legacy alive. They are completely content not to be making a name for themselves. They are known to God, they are loved by Him, and their eternal legacy will be that of belonging to the company of virgins who belong exclusively to God, now and for eternity.

---

1 The word "community" is used throughout the book to mean institute or association, because it is the most familiar term used among us. As you discern, you will inquire about the status of the particular group you are discerning (Association of the Faithful, Diocesan Right, or Pontifical Right) but these distinctions are not helpful to our purposes with this book.

2 A youth ministry program for the children in our East Harlem neighborhood

3 Our Saturday Soup Kitchen was named after Blessed Solanus Casey, Cap., who once lived next door to Our Lady Queen of Angels Convent on 113th Street.

The word "vocation" means "calling." In being called by God, He places a claim on your life, not unlike Adam naming the creatures of the earth. Adam saw each one, knew what it was, and named each according to its true identity. God sees you and calls you according to your true identity.[4] This identity has been yours from the beginning of your existence, but like a seed planted in the soil, it remains hidden until the appointed time. Responding to your vocation is becoming yourself—discovering the person you are meant to be according to the mind and heart of the Father—your Origin and your End.

It is not the intention of this book to unveil the mystery of the religious life for your inspection. No, the life of a religious is necessarily shrouded in mystery. Even the religious sister herself cannot reason away the enigma of the call. Mysterious though it is, the story of this unique call, to a closer following of Jesus Christ as a religious, must be told. God is still calling women to receive this gift, this ancient legacy, but it is increasingly difficult to hear and interpret that call in our modern world with all its many distractions and with the decreased visibility of religious sisters.

If you are a young woman, serious about your faith and trying to be open to a possible call, this book was written for you. It was written especially for those who have never met a religious sister in person, nor have had the opportunity to

---

4 I first heard this insight into the meaning of vocation from Fr. Michael Scanlan, T.O.R. (1931-2017), who was president of Franciscan University of Steubenville when I was a student there in the 1990s. Fr. Michael wrote an excellent work on the topic of discernment entitled *What Does God Want? A Practical Guide to Making Decisions* (Our Sunday Visitor).

sit down for a real heart-to-heart on matters of prayer, vocation, and God-centered decision-making. This book is not a theological treatise on religious life; it is not a substitute for personal spiritual direction. It is a book written from the personal experiences of religious women today. It is a practical manual on how to actively discern religious life, overcome fears, and surmount obstacles.

The majority of Americans grow up around married people. We see marriage and family at its best and at its worst. We see the good and the bad, and we know what it is, and why it is, and we don't need much outside encouragement to desire it. Not so with the religious life. Many Catholics grow up without knowing sisters. For nearly two generations now *The Sound of Music* and *Sister Act* have been just about our only reference point for religious life. Thankfully, despite our ignorance, God is still calling.

One sister I know had the following experience. Already as a high school student, she had begun to pray regularly before the Blessed Sacrament, and soon she began to feel that God was calling her to something special. When the time came for her to consider colleges, she chose a well-known Catholic university. At this new phase of her life, she continued praying on a regular basis, becoming a frequent visitor to a little Eucharistic chapel. After some weeks in regular prayer, in her growing friendship with God, she knew in her heart that God was inviting her to be a religious sister. Perplexed, she responded quite sincerely to God, "How can you be calling me to something that doesn't exist anymore?"

This well-educated, "good Catholic girl," attending a famous Catholic institution, sincerely thought religious life belonged to a bygone era, and if it was not entirely extinct, was getting close to it. Happily, a fine Jesuit priest took her under his wing and corrected her thinking by introducing her to a vibrant young religious community. So began her discernment journey. After visiting several communities, she found her way to the community she would later join, and I can joyfully report that her search ended when she made her final profession of vows in 2010. As a vocation director, when I heard Sr. Elizabeth's story, it lit a fire within me. If "good Catholic girls" are growing up thinking religious life is destined only for a chapter in the history books, we religious sisters are responsible, at least in part. We've got to put this "light on a hill," I thought.

How essential it is to make this beautiful life seen and understood! How else will young people ever be able to give it serious consideration? This book is an effort to contribute to a culture of discernment, to provide a glimpse into the experience of being called by God to something counter-cultural, challenging, and deeply fulfilling: consecration by public vows of poverty, chastity, and obedience in imitation of Jesus Christ and at the service of His Church.

This book was written to fill a very specific need. As you may know, many retreat movements have adopted the custom of ending the retreat with a "vocation call." This is an opportunity for the young retreatants, who are open to the possibility of priesthood or the religious life, to stand up before their peers and to receive a special blessing. For some time now, young men who stand up for the vocation call at Youth 2000 and other retreats, are given the excellent work on discerning the priesthood, *To Save A Thousand Souls*, by

Fr. Brett Brannen. The girls, however, had no such resource to guide them. Finally, I responded to the inner nudge to do something to try to help girls in their discernment. The result was a fourteen-page booklet entitled *Is This A Call?* The booklet is now being distributed free of charge at Youth 2000 retreats and at Steubenville Youth Conferences across the country. It soon became clear that more was needed, and this book is an effort to meet that need for more guidance for young women beginning to experience the still, small voice of a call.

In the chapters ahead you will read about discerning religious life from the perspective of real experience. You'll read the true stories of women who experienced a call, responded, and then made the journey toward religious life. You'll get a step-by-step plan for discernment, an inside scoop on what vocation directors are looking for in applicants, insight into what constitutes readiness to enter religious life, and what you ought to be looking for in a religious community. You will get answers to the most commonly asked questions about the discernment process, as well as precious pearls of advice that sisters have received along their own path, so that you can benefit from the collected wisdom which has already helped real women, not unlike you, to make concrete choices they do not regret.

Naturally, there will be an autobiographical thread running through the text. My own personal experience of discernment, along with the experience of the many women I have accompanied through the years, has been woven through the chapters of this book. The sisters cited span a wide breadth of backgrounds, temperaments, and interests, so that through the variety you will more readily see the religious life as a viable possibility for your own life. These sisters are religious from several different communities, including my own. I opted not to put the community letters behind the sisters' names because it seemed cumbersome and unnecessary.

This book is not meant to promote any one religious community, not even my own! It is meant to help you discern if the religious life is God's will for you. It will give you the tools needed to discover the specific religious community He has prepared for you. It will help you open your heart and receive the gift He is offering you. If He is calling you to belong exclusively to Him, it is for your joy and for His glory. In His will is your peace.

Chapter One

The First
Stirrings of a Call

It is a dramatic image: four women lying face down before the altar. Without knowing anything about religious life, the Catholic Church, or even the Gospel, the symbolism is unmistakable. Clothed in a timeless gray habit and black veil, with a knotted cincture[5] and bare feet,[6] these women turn heads. And even though the congregation is meant to be chanting the Litany of the Saints, and we do, we cannot help but cast a glance to the center aisle to gaze upon the motionless, rock-like figures of the sisters, which speak of surrender and freedom, humility and strength.

It takes anywhere from seven to nine years to get to this

---

5 A cincture is a rope worn around the waist with three knots symbolizing the three vows of poverty, chastity, and obedience, worn by all Franciscans.

6 Sandals are part of the habit of the Franciscan Sisters of the Renewal; however, the sisters traditionally remove their sandals and approach the altar with unshod feet at the time of their vows. As the Lord told Moses, "Remove the sandals from your feet, for the place where you stand is holy ground" (Ex. 3:5).

point: final vows. And for every religious sister, it begins with the first stirring of a call. But how did these women get to this point of laying down their lives, professing life-long vows, which unite them in a new and unique bond to Christ and His Church?

Sr. John Paul Marie is from Eden Prairie, Minnesota. She is one of five children and has a brother who is a Franciscan priest. Sr. John Paul was a neonatal intensive care nurse before entering the convent. Her story begins early. She remembers a vivid dream she had when she was five or six years old. In the dream, St. John Paul II (the pope at the time) said to her, "Do something good for your convent." She knew from that time forward that her call was to be a religious sister. Not that this call wasn't dormant for a time as adolescence set in. Her call was resisted, tested, tried, and all but forgotten. But much later in life, after her education was completed and her nursing career was underway, the restlessness which often precedes a serious time of discernment ultimately led her to the vocation she had been sure of at a tender age. She found that to be a religious sister was, in fact, her true calling.

The first stirrings of a call aren't only reserved for childhood. For some, God chooses adolescence as the moment to make His whisperings heard, like in the case of Sr. Ann Kateri. She was born in New York but grew up in Bethesda, Maryland, the oldest of twelve children, and went on to graduate from Harvard. She was around eleven or twelve years old when the interior sense of being called to "something different" began to emerge for her. It was singing the popular hymn "Here I Am Lord" that helped crystallize her sense of being called. The line "Whom shall I send?" struck her deeply. It was as if the Lord were speaking an invitation just to her. This song took on a personal meaning, and she sang the words from her heart alone in her room at night. It became like a secret promise to God; she knew she would be a sister someday, but not yet.

For Sr. Chiara, an Italian-American from New Jersey, the idea of religious life first entered her consciousness through the suggestion of another. She has a vivid memory of being fifteen years old and drying breakfast dishes with her mother in the kitchen when, out of the blue, her mother said, "Grandma says you're going to be a nun." Her response was, "I don't think so. I want to have a family." Only a few weeks later, while attending a retreat for young people called "Rejoice 2000,"[7] Sr. Chiara surprised her twin sister, and herself, when she stood up for the vocation call at the conclusion of the retreat. Remembering the moment in the kitchen, her mother's announcement of her grandmother's prophecy, Sr. Chiara stood up! "I did think about it—for a minute," she mused. Standing in a gym filled with her peers, she felt a profound peace come over her, and as she walked to the altar to be blessed by the priest, she experienced an unexpected flood of tears. From that moment on, she tucked the thought of being a sister into the back of her mind and let school, sports, and friends take the forefront of her attention. She was just beginning her sophomore year of high school, after all.

---

7 Rejoice 2000 is a retreat modeled after the popular youth retreat called Youth 2000, which exposes Catholic teens to a possibility of a personal relationship with Jesus through the Sacraments of the Catholic Church.

Sr. Veronica has been a sister for over ten years and exhibits a contagious enthusiasm for life. Steubenville, Ohio, was her family's home when they weren't on the road with their traveling ministry, leading parish missions and Holy Hours around the country. She was already a college student, and she was taking a semester abroad when she experienced the grace of a call. The study-abroad program afforded lots of extra travel time, and Sr. Veronica was visiting Paris. While at the Basilica of the Sacred Heart of Jesus, where adoration of the Blessed Sacrament has been happening uninterruptedly for over one hundred thirty years, Sr. Veronica was suddenly aware of a sister in a black, full habit and long black veil. Interiorly, she heard the question distinctly, "Would you live that life for Me?" Sr. Veronica thought she would indeed like to live "that life" for Him, and the thought filled her with deep joy. A question she had long asked had been answered. Jesus was proposing and she said yes!

Sr. Mary Alma is a sister in a teaching community in the Midwest. Her experience was a bit more like a bolt than a whisper. She described her "proposal" like this:

> I was a junior at the University of Nebraska in
> Lincoln and was walking up the street to go
> swimming at Mable Lee Hall on campus. I used
> to like to swim for some exercise. I don't think I
> was praying as I walked. I don't even remember
> thinking of anything in particular. Suddenly, in
> a moment which could not have lasted more
> than two seconds, I experienced something of
> the living Person of Jesus. It was small, like the
> touch of one finger or a drop of dew and yet

it penetrated into my very soul. I remember gasping with joy and then not knowing what to do with myself. I kept saying over and over to myself, "He's real! He's real!" I couldn't contain myself and I started to run toward the Catholic Newman Center on campus. On the way I met one of my sorority sisters, a true friend. Excitedly I told her, "Debbie, I am going to become a nun!" She replied, "That's great! I can see it in you!" Now higher than cloud nine, I ran on to the Catholic Newman Center to tell our priest, Monsignor Leonard Kalin, that I wanted to be a sister. I was so happy. I could not get over the fact that Jesus had asked me to be His. How did He ask me? I cannot say, I can only say that He did. He did not use words, and I did not see Him, but I experienced Him. I did not even have to think much about the response. I ran with joy and certainty. I could not get over the fact that I had such a happy life ahead of me, a life for Him and with Him just like in my dreams. For about two months after this touch from God, I would wake up in the night laughing. I just could not contain the joy that I was going to be His. Six months later, I entered my community.

God decides how the revelation of His will comes about, and it is unique to each.

For me, the first glimmer of a call was during a Sunday night Highlife meeting. Highlife was the non-denominational high school youth group which I faithfully attended. We were living at Benjamin Franklin Village, the Army post in Mannheim, Germany. I think I was a junior at the time. The topic was from the Gospel of Luke, chapter ten, the story of the rich young man. This particular evening, we sat in a circle and discussed the Scripture. This was not the usual youth group format, but this night, this unforgettable night, Scripture was the only fare, and it had an everlasting effect on me. After youth group was over, I went home, still ruminating over the story of that young man and Jesus's words to him: "Sell what you have and give the money to the poor and come follow me." It was so clearly literal, and that poor rich man couldn't do it. I felt a deep uneasiness. What if Jesus was asking me to do this? What if He wanted me to get rid of everything, right now, and actually do what He said to the young man in the Scriptures? I don't know how many hours I spent that night weighing these words and their possible implications in my mind, but I remember it as my first sleepless night. I didn't think of religious life at that point, but just of giving away my belongings and following Jesus.

The Lord is endlessly creative in the means He uses to whisper His will into our souls. Whether it is a dream, a prophetic grandmother, or a mysterious nun, He has His ways! From this side of the convent door, I can look back through the calendar of years and identify many moments along the way, even before the unforgettable youth group meeting, and even many more moments afterwards, which I now see as glimmers of a call. It requires standing at the right distance from a work of art for it to come into sharper focus.

But what happens *after* these grace-filled moments? Clearly none of the stories cited resulted in an immediate phone call to a convent and setting up an entrance date!

Perhaps as you read these stories, you were trying to calculate the time which elapsed between these mystical, grace-filled moments of inspiration and the actual entering of a religious community. In almost every case, the journey from inspiration to decision was many years. In fact, very often the first stirrings of a call did not even initiate a time of conscious, deliberate discernment. Just like a seed planted beneath the soil disappears from sight and growth takes place unseen by anyone but God, so it is with a vocation planted deeply in the heart of a young woman. Much water and sunlight are needed to bring the seed to growth.

Chapter Two

The Agony of Discernment

"I know the plans I have in mind for you, says the Lord, plans for your welfare, not for woe, plans for a future full of hope."

~Jeremiah 29:11

gony. This is the word I most often use to describe my own discernment journey. It's no exaggeration, and I think it somehow consoles other young women who are in the throes of their own tumultuous discernment. Often, when sharing my story, there are knowing looks and nods of empathetic understanding. I freely admit that I did everything wrong in my discernment! St. Paul tells us to boast of our weaknesses, after all. I have come to be grateful for the path I forged, even if it was confusing and difficult, simply because it stands as yet further proof that God's purpose will not be thwarted by our missteps, confusion, ignorance, blunders, and at times, sheer stupidity. Proof can be found in Paul's consoling words to the Romans, "God works all things for good for those who love him, who are called according to his purpose (8:28)."

When I say, "I did everything wrong in my discernment," clearly I had no idea at the time what a blundering mess I was making of it. It's not that I wasn't praying or sincerely trying to trust Him; I just had no idea what I was doing. It wasn't until I started college at the Franciscan University of Steubenville that the notion really sank into my consciousness that there was a plan for my life which did not originate in me. I had been a practicing Catholic all my life, thanks to my parents, who were both converts and very devout. I had already had a "conversion" or "awakening" experience of sorts. I was praying regularly, and I was serious about my faith. Of course, I realized that I didn't just *happen*, that I was created intentionally by God, but the natural corollary to this truth had escaped my consideration: that nothing gets created without a purpose in mind, most especially people, who are the crowning jewel of creation. I am not claiming that I was never taught this, or that no one ever told me that God made me with a purpose in mind, but for whatever reason, if I had heard it, it just didn't sink in. I guess I was not yet very reflective at this point in my life. I was not making decisions based on what I thought God might want; I was having a hard enough time trying to make decisions based on what I thought I wanted. This journey of figuring out what God had in mind when He created me was the beginning of my discernment.

At Steubenville, discernment is in the air![8] You can

---

8 Franciscan University of Steubenville is an apostolate of the Franciscan T.O.R. friars, who are based in Loreto, PA. The Franciscan Sisters of the Sorrowful Mother and Penance, T.O.R. were founded in Steubenville and are a vibrant presence on campus along with the friars.

start discerning without even realizing it's happening to you. Everybody is discerning something: discerning classes, discerning the priesthood, discerning whether to join a household, discerning going to Austria for a semester, discerning whom to take to the Spring Formal, discerning whether to go to The Italian Oven or the Cáfe for dinner. You'll accuse me of exaggeration, but anyone who has been a member of the student body at Franciscan University can confirm this! And so, by the sheer power of suggestion, and almost against my will, I began discerning religious life.

Part of the reason for this pervasive "auto-discernment" is that at Franciscan University there are religious everywhere: teaching classes, taking classes, on campus, off campus, and even living in the dorms. The Sisters of Saint Francis of the Martyr Saint George,[9] or "The Martyrs," lived on the fourth floor of Tommy More (St. Thomas More Residence Hall) all four years of my college career. I found it interesting to observe them from afar, although I made it a point to not speak to them. With all of these realities converging upon me (a new awareness that God had a plan for my life, the strong religious presence on campus, and the pervasive "discernment pressure"), one might think I would be on discernment easy-street. Where does the "agony" come in?

---

9 The Sisters of Saint Francis of the Martyr Saint George were founded in Germany and are based in Alton, Illinois. Their charism is seeking to make the merciful love of Christ known, and they do this primarily through teaching and nursing. The sisters both taught and studied at F.U.S. while I was there, and I know that their presence had an effect on my desire to be open to religious life.

The word "discernment" was wielded lightly in my new environment, with no clear definition. Discernment was like a vague notion of openness, or even attempted openness; or in my case, if truth be told, total closed-ness with a desire to *seem* open in order to fit in to my pious surroundings.[10] Thus, when someone asked if I was discerning (and they did ask; this was Steubenville after all), I would respond, "Yes, I am open to God's will." Looking back on this response now, with the benefit of the years, I can see how untrue it was. In fact, I was not open. I was scared to death of being called to religious life. I desperately hoped that God's plans were identical to mine and therefore included marriage, children, and mission work. An honest response would have been, "No, I'm not discerning. I don't really know what discernment is or how one goes about it. But I am getting the idea that God has a plan, some sort of special mission for me, and while that seems exciting and I would like to discover it, I am scared. Being here, among so many religious, brings that possibility to the forefront of my mind, but honestly, I hope God has other plans for me, because the pictures in my mind that go along with religious life are somber, rigid, and the whole possibility of it is dreadfully intimidating."

Unfortunately, I was nowhere near able to make such an honest response, largely because I was not yet self-reflective

---

10 I imagine that there were plenty of people at Steubenville with a more advanced understanding of discernment than me, and I do not mean to project my ignorance onto the entire student body. Koinonia Household, for example, was always brimming full of men discerning the priesthood, and I suspect that they were truly engaged in an authentic, prayerful, well-guided process of discernment. Nonetheless, I expect that my experience was not uncommon.

enough to get at that truth *myself*, let alone to articulate it to anybody else. And so the conflict began. I was beginning to realize that happiness would only come in doing God's will, but I knew I was asking a question with an answer I may not have liked, and the thought of giving up my plans was excruciating to me.

I'll pause here in the telling of my tale to insert some further hindsight. I can see now that I was in no way ready to discern religious life (even if I would have had a proper understanding of what discernment was), for several reasons. My friendship with God had not developed to the point of a deep and authentic trust yet. The idea to discern was not coming from within, a fruit of prayer, a response to the whisperings of the Spirit; rather, it was somewhat forced and artificial, to say the least. I didn't have a good intellectual understanding of what I was even attempting to discern. Even though I lived in close proximity to religious sisters, there was no way you would ever find me talking to them! God forbid I get labeled a "future nun!" My chances of getting asked to Spring Formal would be hopelessly dashed!

In short, the basic prerequisites for authentic discernment were absent. I lacked what St. Ignatius calls "indifference," that detachment which makes a person truly available to God. Indifference is the virtue a soldier has as he awaits orders. It doesn't matter so much what those orders are; he is in a state of internal equilibrium which allows him to be led.

My discernment journey is living proof that when you are in the state of grace and trying to figure out the way forward, God will not abandon you. As pathetic as my initial attempts at following Him were, He didn't leave me wandering in the desert! He searched me out and found me; He captured me, and I will be grateful for this all my days! He wanted me to discover happiness and joy within my true vocation even more than I did! Even though I have experienced God's ability to salvage a discernment gone wrong, I know now that there is an easier way. It wasn't meant to be so hard!

To continue the drama of my discernment, my mistakes were not limited to the beginning of the process; in fact, they carried straight through until my practically miraculous and very happy entrance into the long-evaded religious life. I never had a spiritual director, and I never spoke to a sister about my fears and misconceptions. I dated, fell in love, and tried to discern religious life all at the same time. And finally, I didn't even visit any convents (except the one I ultimately entered). Basically, if you do the opposite of everything I did, on each point, you will have a much different tale to tell, and a much smoother journey, guaranteed! Discernment should be much less an "agony" and much more an "adventure," much less a feeling of pressure and much more a feeling of being lovingly pursued. For God Himself is pursuing you. He is searching for you. Will you let yourself be found?

Chapter Three

Friendship with God

C an you imagine starting a relationship with someone by taking him by the shoulders and exclaiming, "Am I supposed to marry you?" If he doesn't break free and run away, he might respond, "How about we go out for coffee first before we start planning the wedding?" Discernment of a religious vocation sometimes starts like that! We want to throttle God for an answer to our vocation before we ever even pause to try to get to know Him. Your relationship with God is of utmost importance. You should be a friend before you become a spouse.

I can remember when I went from simply being Catholic to beginning a friendship with God. From before the time I could speak, I knew our family was Catholic. We wouldn't dream of missing Mass on Sunday. Naturally, we prayed before meals, said the occasional rosary, and went to CCD.[11] The idea, however, of friendship with God, of knowing God,

---

11 Confraternity of Christian Doctrine (CCD) was the catechetical program for Catholic children who didn't attend Catholic school.

of a back-and-forth, give-and-take, living communion with Almighty God had not ever occurred to me until my freshman year of high school when I attended a youth retreat at the strong encouragement of my parents. We were living at Fort Campbell, Kentucky, home of the Army's 101 Airborne Division, and a group of parents who had been touched by the Charismatic Renewal were eager to pass the fire on to the younger generation. They could see the problem clearly. We were Catholic kids. We went to Mass dutifully every Sunday. We even went to CCD. But were we Christians? That is, were we sincere followers of Jesus, people who knew Him, and in freedom were choosing to follow Him?

On the second night of the retreat, the parents who planned the weekend each got on the microphone and shared their personal stories. I remember sitting in the very back row shrouded in attitude, as only a teenager can muster, masking my profound interest behind my crossed arms and one raised eyebrow. From inside my armor, I was listening intently. In each person who spoke, I heard common elements. They spoke very personally, out of their own real life experience. They were honest and vulnerable. This was neither a lecture nor a history lesson, and it certainly wasn't CCD. And what did they share? They shared about Jesus Christ and who He was to them; how He was involved in their lives; how they experienced Him bearing their burdens with them. I had never heard anyone speak about Jesus as if He were a real person, alive and well, a person that could be known and befriended, listened to, and followed.

The result of this retreat was that a new idea entered my mind. And the idea was this: It might be possible to actually know God. The idea led to a question: Is it possible for me to really know Him? The question led to a desire, and the desire to prayer. "God, if it is possible to know You, I want to know You."

It is no exaggeration to credit that weekend and the witness of those charismatic parents who organized the retreat with changing my life forever. I went home a different person. I remember going to Sunday Mass afterwards and listening to every word and watching every action on the altar. I was scrutinizing the Mass. Is this true? Is this what I believe? I can remember praying the Creed in particular, hearing myself say every article and questioning myself as I did so: do you really believe this in the depths of your heart? And I knew then that the answer was, "Yes. Yes, I do believe." I could now say: "This is my faith."

After the retreat, I began attending a charismatic prayer meeting with my sister Maria (which was mostly made up of people our parents' age), and I also started to try to pray on my own and to read the Bible. I started at the beginning with Genesis (even though everybody says not to do that) and I read the whole thing cover-to-cover as an exercise of sheer determination. I understood little and pondered less. But I read it. I was trying to familiarize myself with God's Word because I wanted to familiarize myself with God.[12]

How do you begin a friendship with someone you can't see? A divine Someone? I had heard that praying every day

---

12 A more helpful approach would have been to start with the New Testament, in particular with Matthew, Mark, Luke, and John. An excellent biblical commentary is the *Navarre Series* (University of Navarre), which was inspired by St. Josemaria Escriva.

was a good idea. So I tried to take time to pray every day, with greater or lesser success throughout my high school years. I began praying by writing out my prayers in a journal: "Dear God..." This was an easier starting point than maintaining the conversation mentally. Between pouring out my heart on paper, reading His inspired Word, and continuing to attend Mass every Sunday, I was beginning a relationship with God, the start of a real friendship.

Sometimes young women are tempted to ask the question about a call to religious life before they have begun this journey of friendship with God. Maybe having attended a powerful weekend retreat, or after a mission trip, the question of a religious vocation is suddenly there, urging a response. Sometimes at the suggestion of a priest or a parent, religious life suddenly becomes a question that needs answering. But genuine discernment flows from relationship, just like deciding to marry someone flows from falling in love with him.

Do you have a relationship with God? Do you spend time with Him regularly? Do you know that He loves you? Not just that He *is* Love, but that He loves *you*. You personally. God is looking on you with love right this minute as you read this book. He sees you, He knows you and He loves you. His gaze is always on you. It always was, and it always will be, a loving gaze. This is the starting point, not just of religious life, but of Christian life.

If, as you read this, you realize you are asking the question about vocation without a relationship with God, I recommend putting your vocational discernment on the back burner and investing your time and energy in forming a friendship with God. Regular Mass, frequent Confession, and personal prayer time, especially with the Scriptures, are pillars of a strong friendship with the Lord.

The following outline is a tried-and-true method for praying with Scripture as popularized by St. Ignatius. This method utilizes the imagination. The ability to visualize the biblical scenes and to hear, smell, and touch, all with your interior senses, is essential for this prayer. If you don't have a vivid imagination, a more classic style of Lectio Divina may be a better method for you.[13]

> **Step 1:** Decide how long your prayer period will be and then be faithful to the amount of time you decide on. Find a quiet place to pray where you won't be interrupted. Settle into a quiet, recollected mindset. Place yourself in the presence of God, perhaps with the Sign of the Cross and a prayer to the Holy Spirit.
>
> **Step 2:** Ask for the grace you seek. For example: "I pray for the grace to know and trust God as a loving Father." "I pray for the grace to know and believe in the love God has for me." "I pray for the grace to grow in a genuine trusting relationship with the God Who loves me." "I pray for the grace to know what God wants me to do and for the courage to do it." Pray for the grace you seek in your own words. You may desire to pray for the same grace for days or weeks or

---

13 See Appendix B for an outline of Lectio Divina.

months until you have received it.

Step 3: Read through the Scripture passage you selected to pray with, perhaps the Gospel read at daily Mass or a passage selected for help in discernment. Read the Scripture again to familiarize yourself with the passage and to construct the scene in your mind's eye.

Step 4: Use your imagination and place yourself in the scene. Let your imagination go and allow the story to unfold. Let the Lord speak directly to you using the Scriptures. Try to pray with the heart, not just the mind. Repeat steps 3 and 4 for the amount of prayer time you decided upon.

Step 5: Have a heart-to-heart conversation with Our Lady, or Jesus, or the Father, or the Holy Spirit about whatever is coming up in your prayer. This is called a colloquy, or a spiritual conversation.

Step 6: End your prayer time with an Our Father or another prayer.

Step 7: After your designated time for prayer is over, either immediately or later on, it is a good practice to review your prayer. This means thinking back over your prayer time and asking the question, "What happened during prayer? What were the feelings that stirred during prayer? Did I receive the grace I prayed for?"

> Many people find it helpful to write the results
> of their review of prayer in a journal.

Growing in your relationship with God will never be time wasted. It is from this place of personal relationship that your vocation will come.

If He is calling you to consecrated life, you don't have to worry about the call going away because you set the question aside for a time. As St. Augustine famously said, "Our hearts are restless until they rest in Thee." The call will be there and it will grow.

Your prayer, by the time you are considering making convent visits, should include longstanding sacramental practice. The holy sacrifice of the Mass is the highest and greatest prayer we have. It is a basic requirement of our faith, and a tremendous privilege, to participate in Holy Mass every Sunday. If you are discerning, you may want to try to go to Mass even more often, perhaps even daily, if you can find one that fits into your schedule. Allowing the sacraments to take a greater place in your spiritual life will allow you opportunities for real contact with God—Father, Son, and Holy Spirit. The sacraments are the means by which God forms His children. At Mass, He instructs us through His Word. If we are paying attention, we get ancient history, sociology, anthropology, and poetry. More importantly we hear God speaking directly to us—all in the inspired Word of God proclaimed at Mass through the cycle of readings. The Word of God is a permanent presence by which God remains among us. It is meant to transform and guide our lives. Furthermore, we receive the nourishment of the Body and Blood of Christ. God Himself becomes our food. The Eucharist unites us physically and spiritually to Christ, to other Christians, and to the heavenly Liturgy. This is an unfathomable mystery, and we must always be on guard against becoming numbed by routine or taking Him for granted.

The Sacrament of Reconciliation (or Confession) is also a great help to spiritual growth. In this sacrament, we meet God's never-ending mercy. This is an opportunity not only to be forgiven, but also to be healed and to reestablish our relationship to the Church because our sins have an effect which goes beyond self. Confession is a concrete way to experience ongoing conversion. This conversion, healing, forgiveness, and restored communion with the Church, puts us in a good position to go forward in our vocation because it keeps us humble and grounded in reality. The Catechism explains, "The confession (or disclosure) of sins, even from a simply human point of view, frees us and facilitates our reconciliation with others. Through such an admission man looks squarely at the sins he is guilty of, takes responsibility for them, and thereby opens himself again to God and to the communion of the Church in order to make a new future possible" (CCC 1423).

Along with steeping yourself in the sacraments, Eucharistic adoration is also a great means of deepening your friendship with God and preparing yourself for your vocation. The following are true stories of the impact of having a commitment to Eucharistic adoration.

When Sr. Mary Pietà was a college student at Benedictine College in Atchison, Kansas, and still unsure of her own call, she suffered a deep loss when her best friend left college mid-stream to enter a religious community. Even though she was happy for her friend, the loss was real and left a deep impact on her. This is when she decided to start going daily to Eucharistic adoration. At first, she went primarily to grieve the loss of her friend. But as the pain of loss began to subside, Sr. Mary Pietà continued to meet Our Lord in adoration each day, and a real friendship was developing. It wasn't as if she had an abundance of free time and easily added adoration to a light schedule. She was a double major, student teaching, and serving as a resident assistant. Yet, busy as she was, she began to make Eucharistic adoration a priority in her life. The intimacy that developed between Sr. Mary Pietà and the Lord in adoration became the wellspring of life for her that carried her through her own vocational discernment and continues to this day as a perpetually professed sister.

Sr. John Paul too credits her many hours of Eucharistic adoration as the source of grace needed to hear, understand, and accept her call with joy. Sr. John Paul was working as an intensive care nurse in Fort Myers, Florida, living with good friends, traveling and living her single life to the full before settling down into her vocation. She was happy and fulfilled on all counts, except she hadn't met the right man to marry yet. This was a source of frustration and growing anxiety for her. Her parish in Florida had a perpetual adoration chapel, and she started to go there regularly. At first, she went for a specific purpose, to pray for a husband! And sure enough, she did begin to fall in love—with Our Lord, truly present in the Blessed Sacrament. It didn't take long for the vocation she had literally dreamed of as a child to become clear and undeniable. Sr. John Paul professed her final vows with three other sisters on June 6, 2016.

"It is impossible to exaggerate the close relation between the Holy Eucharist and the vocation to the priesthood and religious life," wrote Fr. John Harden, S.J. In fact, he asserted that the Eucharist is the best way to foster vocations: "Persons who attend Mass, receive Communion, and invoke Christ in the Blessed Sacrament obtain light and strength that no one else has a claim to."[14]

Our relationship with God, like our other relationships, is meant to grow and change throughout life. Surely your relationship with your mother and father is very different today than it was when you were in second grade. Investing time and energy into your relationship with God is a needed predisposition to discernment.

---

14   Fr. John Harden, S.J., www.therealpresence.org/archives/Religious_
Life/Religious_Life_037.htm

Chapter Four

Discerning With Our Lady

In my own vocation story, the breakthrough came when I hit a wall. Suddenly the obvious truth finally occurred to me that I was getting nowhere in my discernment. I was twenty-four years old, doing work that I loved, dating on and off, and feeling called but confused. I remember that suddenly my plight seemed urgent. I was making no progress. What would become of my life? Would I *ever* be clear enough about *anything* to make a decision?

I had been going to Eucharistic adoration at St. Bonaventure's Church in Troy, Ohio, a few towns away from where I was living. My prayer was, "Give me clarity, Lord. Please make it crystal-clear so that I can act." I knew enough to know I could not make a decision so big while still enveloped in a fog of uncertainty. I'll admit I felt a certain urgency and even desperation. I had a growing confidence that I was quite capable of ruining my life, and I knew I needed some help. Finally, I did what I should have done from the beginning: I turned to Our Lady.

It was May, Our Lady's month, in 1998, the year

dedicated to the Holy Spirit,[15] when I turned to her for guidance. In my prayer, I imagined myself as an infant, utterly helpless, in the arms of Our Blessed Mother. "Carry me to the Father's will," I prayed. "I can't do this by myself." Finally a moment of truth! I really did not know anything, and at last, I had sense enough to reach out for help from one who is ever ready and ever able to give it.

There is plenty of evidence that Mary, the mother of Jesus, can and does assist us. Biblically, we have the events at the famous wedding in Cana which offer a touching example of Our Lady's special concern for the couple; in them we can see ourselves, ill-prepared, yet not without Our Lady's special concern.

In *The Mother of the Redeemer*, St. John Paul II describes how the Church sees Mary's role with us:

> [The Church] sees Mary deeply rooted in humanity's history, in man's eternal vocation according to the providential plan which God has made for him from eternity. She sees Mary maternally present and sharing in the many complicated problems which today beset the lives of individuals, families and nations; she sees her helping the Christian people in the constant struggle between good and evil, to ensure that it 'does not fall', or if it has fallen, that it 'rises again'.[16]

---

15   Pope John Paul II dedicated the years leading up to the Great Jubilee Year of 2000 to the Father, the Son, and the Holy Spirit. The grace I received was on Pentecost Sunday in the year dedicated to the Holy Spirit. No coincidence.

16   *Redemptoris Mater*, 52.

Add to that the further evidence of modern history in which so often Our Lady has appeared with serious warnings and eternally helpful advice. Perhaps my favorite demonstration of Our Lady's special desire to help us was given to St. Catherine Labouré. Catherine was a novice at the time that she experienced a visit from the Blessed Mother. It was July 18, 1830. First, Sr. Catherine is awoken in the middle of the night by a beautiful little child who instructs her to go to the chapel to meet a special visitor. She springs up, dresses in her full habit and veil, and obeys the child. Waiting in the chapel for some time, at last she hears something. It is the rustling of silk as Our Lady arrives in the sanctuary. Mary seats herself on a chair, and Sr. Catherine approaches, kneeling beside her and laying her head on Mary's lap, as they hold a conversation which lasted over two hours! Among other things, Our Lady said, "Come to the foot of the altar. There graces will be shed upon all, great and little, who ask for them. Graces will be especially shed on those who ask for them."[17]

On another visit, Mary stands with arms outstretched and rays of light shining down to earth through the gems on her fingers. When asked by Sr. Catherine the meaning of the gems emitting rays of light, and likewise, the meaning of the gems which have no rays of light, Our Lady explained that the gems with light signify the graces flowing to those who ask for them. The gems without the light represent graces no one is asking for. Our Lady also asked that a medal be struck depicting this scene and inscribed with the prayer, "O Mary

---

17   The details of the apparitions of St. Catherine Labouré can be found in the book by Fr. Joseph I. Dirvin: *Saint Catherine Labouré of the Miraculous Medal* (TAN, 1984).

conceived without sin, pray for us who have recourse to thee." We call this the Miraculous Medal, an apt nickname as so many favors and true miracles have come about through Our Lady's hands, for those who heed her open invitation to come to her for special help.

The message of available grace, free help, assistance from on high, sounds almost too good to be true. Once the truth of this reality sinks in, you realize there is a powerful advantage on your side: a mother who happens to be the Queen of Heaven and Earth, who *lives* to assist her children! Truly this is a knowledge that changes things for anyone who believes.

I had my own vivid experience of Our Lady's powerful assistance. Within one month of turning to her for vocational help, I had the answer to my prayer. I was attending a young adult conference with some friends. It was Pentecost Sunday, the last Sunday in May that year, and a crowd of more than a thousand was gathered for Mass. I did not have my vocation particularly in mind as Mass began; I was just trying to concentrate and do my best to pray, in spite of the handsome Italian-American attorney sitting to my left. It was the point of the Mass when the priest elevates the Host. In that moment, I looked up at Our Lord held high in the hands of His priest, and I experienced the deepest, most profound sense of *knowing*. What I knew was that Jesus was the *only one* who would satisfy my heart. The significance of this is hard to express adequately. The question of whether or not my heart could truly be satisfied in religious life was the giant obstacle which had prevented me from moving forward. This question was being answered in the affirmative.

Not only that, but I took it as a promise. Jesus was saying to me, "I will satisfy your heart." In that moment, I knew the call that had been placed upon my life. I knew for what I had been made, for Whom I had been made. When the Father had first called me into being, He envisioned me as His, for Himself alone. And finally, I could say yes to this plan. For the first time since the thought of religious life had occurred to me, it filled me with joy. This new clarity, this new promise, changed everything.

I immediately remembered my first attraction to the sisters I had met on a pilgrimage to Denver to see Pope John Paul II. I called almost immediately. To my surprise, the mother superior herself answered the phone, and I blurted out my whole story to her from the beginning. Now that the chief obstacle had been removed, my joy and eagerness were boundless. Mother invited me to visit, I purchased a plane ticket for New York, and I just kept going forward from there. In three months, I joined the community as a postulant.

This longed-for grace of clarity and peace came at the intercession of Our Lady. She is the secret that all the saints have found. There is no surer way to travel safely this pilgrimage of life than with one hand in hers.

Sr. Michael Marie also attributes her religious vocation to Our Lady. One day her brother told her matter-of-factly that she was going to be a sister. Sr. Michael resisted his "prophecy" with a curt "We'll see about that." One day, while looking up at the crucifix, she had the piercing revelation: "No one loves me like Him." And she received the grace to say yes to her call. She later found out from her mother that her brother had been praying the rosary for her daily to be able to respond to the Lord's call.

For Sr. Catherine, too, Our Lady played a pivotal role in her vocation journey. When she was sixteen years old, she was sent on a pilgrimage to Fatima with her cousin. On the first day as she entered the shrine, she heard the words interiorly, "You are going to be a sister." What followed was a profound rush of peace and joy. Sr. Catherine was at the beginning of her speed skating career at the time. After the trip to Fatima, in which she consecrated her skating to Our Lady, she went on to break the world record for her age group. She also went on to skate for the U.S. team at the 1998 Winter Olympics in Nagano, Japan. Later she went on to the School of the Art Institute of Chicago, and later still, discerned a religious vocation. She became a perpetually professed sister in 2010—just as Our Lady said she would. Inside Sr. Catherine's ring of final profession is inscribed the words *To Jesus through Mary.* "Mary is and always has been Mother of my vocation," shared Sr. Catherine.

St. John Paul II was a great devotee of Our Lady, taking *Totus Tuus* as his Episcopal motto. (The phrase means "Totally Yours," a two-word condensed formula for Marian consecration.) When he was a young man discerning his priestly vocation and living in Cracow, Poland, he grappled with the same questions many Christians ponder regarding the appropriate emphasis for Marian devotion. Already convinced that Mary leads us to Christ, the future pope began to discover that Christ also leads us to His mother. Still conflicted, he wondered if his own growing Marian devotion could compromise the supremacy of the worship owed to Christ.[18] He found help in the writings of St. Louis Marie de Montfort.[19] Through his study, he became an advocate of the devotion known as "Total Consecration," that is, a total gift of self to Jesus through Mary. This devotion is "the surest, easiest, shortest, and most perfect way of approaching Jesus,"[20] of becoming who you were created to be. Total consecration entails: renouncing the devil, the world, sin and self, as expressed in the act of consecration, and giving oneself entirely to Jesus through Mary.[21]

Total consecration brings a number of profoundly desirable effects. St. Louis de Montfort makes clear the benefits which are received by those who make Mary their Mother through total consecration to Mary:

1. She loves them tenderly
2. Promotes their interests and manages their affairs
3. Gives them excellent advice
4. Prepares them body and soul to be a gift to God
5. Clothes them in virtue and merit
6. Obtains for them the blessing of the Father
7. Provides for their needs
8. Leads and guides them
9. Defends and protects them
10. Intercedes for them

---

18   Pope John Paul II, *Gift and Mystery*, 28

19   *God Alone: The Collected Writings of St. Louis Marie de Montfort* (Montfort Publications), is a comprehensive resource for further reading and preparation for Marian consecration.

20   *True Devotion to Mary*, 55

21   Ibid, 126.

This list describes exactly the help that you need as you seek God's will for your future! Help from heaven is available to you for your discernment journey and for every other need! St. Teresa of Calcutta said, "You cannot learn this from books, you must experience it in your life—that whatever you ask Our Lady she will do!"

Our Lady not only obtains graces for us; she is also a role model of endless inspiration. Think of her Annunciation if you struggle to say yes without foreknowledge of the plan. Think of her visit to Elizabeth when you are feeling selfish and having trouble relinquishing comforts or control. Meditate on Our Lady traveling at nine months pregnant and giving birth in a stable if you wonder how you'll manage the austerities of the convent. Remember the Presentation and the promise of a sword when your own heart is pierced by those who do not understand your call. Consider Mary's three-day search for Jesus when you are enveloped in darkness and have lost all consolation. Further, Our Lady's role does not end with discernment assistance. She does not abandon us at the threshold of the convent to figure the rest out on our own. No, Mother Mary is in fact the model of religious life and the constant companion for all who seek her.[22]

Entrusting both your discernment and your vocation to her protection can be done with a simple, heartfelt Hail Mary. I recommend doing so daily.

---

22 Some formulas for Marian Consecration can be found in Appendix A.

Chapter Five

A Foundation for Discernment

At nineteen years old, when Sr. Veronica first thought she might be called to be a religious sister, she described her emotional reaction in these words: "A great sense of joy, peace, and excitement rushed upon me, like the experience of having been waiting for a loved one to arrive and then suddenly hearing his voice at the door. I was eager to open the door of my heart to this invitation." For others, including me, the first thought of religious life brought a mild sense of dread and provoked resistance. For others, there may be disbelief, awe, joy, uncertainty, shyness, or doubt. Sometimes disappointment, frustration, and anger are rolled up in the emotions attached to the first thought of religious life.

It could be tempting to assume that one emotional reaction is better than another. In fact, we are not in control of our spontaneous, emotional reactions, and there is not a moral value attached to them. However, taking a deeper look at why we react the way we do can be very fruitful and important for our growth.

It's also important to remember that your first reaction isn't the same thing as your final response. First of all, it can take time to even get in touch with your deeper feelings, beneath the surface reactions, beneath the fears.

Well before I had any clarity about my vocation, I saw a film on the Missionaries of Charity with Mother Teresa's voice providing the narration in the background. At one point in the film she says something like, "When a woman is being called to be the spouse of Christ, in her heart she knows it." I remember thinking, "Oh good, I must not be called." Shortly afterwards I thought, "Unless, maybe I am called." And later still, I thought with some annoyance, "How can she come out with such definitive statements like that!" while wondering if it could be true. Her words popped into my mind many times over the years of my discernment. And now all these years later, I can say that I think I finally understand her meaning. The seed of my vocation, the DNA of my true identity, was planted in the soil of my heart and yet hidden from my own sight. Long before I was able to admit it, even to myself, in that deep innermost place, I think I always knew I was called. But I was not *ready* to know. I couldn't handle the knowing. I was not ready to freely choose and joyfully embrace a call to religious life, and so I didn't let myself know what I knew.

There is not a right or wrong emotional response to the idea of a vocation. Your emotional response is what it is. The thinking which gives rise to the emotions is what needs attention. In the first part of my own discernment journey, I was weighing a very rosy, happy, picture-perfect image of marriage against a very bleak, somber, stifling picture of religious life—unreal verses unreal. This was not even the *beginning* of true discernment because I was not yet weighing real against real. The scenario in my mind was not representative of reality. If thinking is the foundation on which the house of your vocation is built, make it rock-solid truth, not the shifting sands of vague impressions and sweeping generalizations.

Let's take another example of the importance of the thinking which gives rise to an emotional response. If the thought of being a religious sister is met with a joyous reaction because I have been hurt in the past by my relationships with men, and therefore I think a religious vocation will minimize the possibility of such hurt from happening again, then I have an area that needs attention. Healing from the past is needed before I can hope to discern well. Perhaps by delving further into an understanding of the Sacrament of Matrimony as something good and beautiful and desirable will also be needed. On the other hand, if the thought of religious life brings on a fearful emotional reaction—because I think I would not make a suitable sister, or because I feel I am not pious enough, or because I think I don't have the right temperament, or because my past makes me feel hypocritical—then there are areas in my thinking that need attention. In both emotional reactions, the thinking has false premises and therefore the starting point for discernment is faulty.

Our emotions do not spring from a vacuum; they most often follow our thinking. If your friend bursts into tears "for no reason" during chemistry class, just ask her what she was *thinking* about right before her outburst. When she reveals that she was remembering that it was the first anniversary of her grandfather's death, you can easily understand her tears. Our emotions follow our thoughts, and if our thoughts are irrational or exaggerated or otherwise faulty, the emotions they lead to can't be trusted or followed.

According to St. Paul, thinking with the mind of Christ is essential to authentic discernment. Paul says to "put on the mind of Christ" so that "you may discern what is the will of God, what is good and pleasing and perfect" (Rom. 12:2). A starting point for discerning a call to religious life, then, is not how we feel about it, as much as what we think about it. Your thinking about God, your thoughts about yourself, and what you know about religious life are critically important as you venture into a time of discernment. Your intellectual formation is essential.[23]

Don't misunderstand my meaning here. I am not placing mind over heart. No, the heart, the deepest core of your inmost self, is indeed to be followed. But the heart is much more than spontaneous emotional reactions. Discernment is best done by "folding the wings of your intellect and placing your head in your heart"[24] and going from there! It is the integration of the two which prepares us to advance. Sr. Chiara expresses well the integration of mind and heart: "The joy that I experienced with this call was different than any other feeling of joy that I've ever had. It was different because

---

23   There are many books cited in the footnotes throughout this work; additionally there is a short reading list in Appendix C.

24   Here I borrow a phrase from one of my favorite spiritual writers, Servant of God Catherine de Hueck Doherty, founder of the secular institute Madonna House. She uses this phrase several times in her classic work on prayer, *Poustinia* (Madonna House Publications).

it sprang from knowing that I was chosen by God who infinitely knows and loves me." Sr. Chiara's deeply-felt joy was a fruit of what she knew; it was her heart's response to the truth.

Let us explore the building blocks of our thinking about God, ourselves, and the religious life to ensure that the soil in which the seed is planted is not toxic but fertile.

The Way I Think about God

Satan's interference with Adam and Eve in the peace and paradise of the garden was fundamentally an attempt to abolish fatherhood.[25] It was truly an audacious aim on his part, and while he can't affect the fatherhood of God directly, he has been tragically successful in affecting our perception of God as a loving father. Satan sowed the seeds of mistrust and fear, and we can find evidence of this original, diabolical plan in our own thinking and lurking under our every sin.

There are many attributes of God, many more unknown than known, but at the core, God is Father. He has revealed Himself as such and in Jesus we see Him and have access to Him. He is a loving father, an interested father, a generous father, and a trustworthy father. And He is *your* father. Your father knows you, He knows everything about you, and He loves you. Have you ever prayed Psalm 139 as if it were written by you to God?

---

25 St. John Paul II explains the attempt to abolish fatherhood as the lens through which to understand the original sin in the book-length interview, *Crossing the Threshold of Hope*, (Alfred A. Knopf), 227-228.

O Lord, you search me and you know me,
you know my resting and my rising,
you discern my purpose from afar.
you mark when I walk or when I lie down,
all my ways lie open to you....

For it was you who created my being,
knit me together in my mother's womb.
I thank you for the wonder of my being,
for the wonders of your creation.

Already you knew my soul,
my body held no secret from you
when I was being fashioned in secret
and molded in the depths of the earth....

O search me, God and know my heart.
O test me and know my thoughts.
See that I follow not the wrong path
and lead me in the path of life eternal.
(Psalm 139: 1-4, 13-15, 23-24)[26]

If your fundamental perception of God is less than that of a loving father, your discernment will be on an unsteady foundation. It is all too common to nurture an image of God as all-seeing, all-knowing, and all-powerful, but also as distant and authoritarian, a judge not a father, a ruler not a lover. In order to trust God and to surrender to Him freely, we

---

26   The Psalm is quoted from The Grail version of the Psalter, as used in the American English translation of the Liturgy of the Hours.

need to know we are in the hands not only of our Maker but of our *Father*—in His safe, loving hands. Why would a father want his child to be unhappy? Yet all too often I meet people who are sure that they will be miserable if they submit to God's plan. This is a disposition I understand well, because I was there myself! I can see now, even though I did not possess this awareness at the time, that my long resistance to religious life was the result of a lack of trust. Luckily, God is very patient. As my relationship with God grew, trust grew. It's not how you start out, but how you end up that matters.

The Way I Think About Myself

Self-image, self-esteem, self-help—the market is flooded with consumer merchandise to improve our image. But we have a perfectly good image: God's image. Every human being was created deliberately, thoughtfully, intentionally by God. You were willed by Him. He called you into being and you are good. In fact, you are *very* good.

There are many reasons that we think we are bad or broken beyond repair. It is not true. God's mercy endures forever, and there is no such thing as an unforgivable sin, except the sin we withhold from His mercy. There is no experience that can't be healed. Our starting point for a proper self-image must be that of child of God: a beloved, wanted child of God. Your Father planned your life and thus He has hopes and dreams *for* your life. He loves you and what He wants for you is for your good and for your joy.

Sometimes as the question of religious life presents itself in a young woman's life, wounds from the past emerge as obstacles. For most young adults, some inner healing is part of the maturing process. Fr. Benedict Groeschel, CFR,[27] was fond of saying that none of us was raised in the Holy Family, and we've all got chips in the furniture to prove it. Perhaps you've seen the cartoon of a "Functional Family Convention." The cartoonist drew a stadium of empty seats. The healing of emotional wounds can most often happen through a regular sacramental life including frequent Mass and regular Confession. In the sacraments of the Church we come into direct and personal contact with the Divine Physician, and healing is a consequence.[28]

The Way I Think About Religious Life

Even though I did not go to Catholic school, and I did not grow up knowing religious sisters, I had a pretty clear image in my mind of what I did not like about religious life. Words that came to mind in connection with it were: rigid, serious, pious, oppressive, difficult, lonely, and unfulfilling. Where did this negative image come from? Wherever it came from, it was not from real life experience with sisters.

In my nearly twenty years of religious life, I can say that the words that spring up for me now at the thought of this

27   Fr. Benedict Groeschel, CFR (1933-2015) was one of the eight founders of the Franciscan Friars of the Renewal. Fr. Benedict was a popular spiritual writer and preacher with a live program on EWTN for many years. He was a father to the poor, great advocate for life, and defender of the outcast. He is renowned for his holiness and practical approach to the spiritual life.

28   Should more assistance be needed, www.catholictherapists.com can help in finding a Catholic therapist in your area. "Unbound" retreats are also a means of finding freedom and healing. Information about retreats and other resources can be found at www.heartofthefather.com.

counsels, we have the prescription for holiness for all the faithful according to their state in life. Our life is meant to resemble His. Jesus became a man, but He also became a Way. The religious life is an effort to conform even *more* radically to the Way, because this is precisely what the religious has been called to do.

This way of life, this consecrated existence known as religious life, is different from other forms of consecration, such as the consecration of those in secular institutes, consecrated virgins, or hermits. The Catechism of the Catholic Church and Canon Law explain what is distinct for religious life: its liturgical character, the public profession of vows, life lived in common, and public witness. By this total offering of self, their whole existence becomes a continuous act of worshiping God in love.[34]

Holy Indifference

If your thinking is clear and correct, and you know yourself to be loved by our good Father in heaven, and you have come to believe that in His goodness, the plan He has for your life is for your joy, you are close to being ready to start discerning because your foundation is growing solid.

The next question you will need to confront is, "Am I detached enough to discern?" To have the proper disposition in discernment you have to be ready for any answer—able to accept "yes" and able to accept "no." If I desperately want to

---

34   *Catechism of the Catholic Church,* paragraph 925, explains religious life as distinct from the universal call to holiness. Canon law 607 highlights the distinctive characteristic of religious life.

get married and have children and can conceive of happiness in no other way, yet I try to discern religious life perhaps out of duty or obligation, I am not really ready for authentic discernment. St. Ignatius referred to the needed disposition as "indifference." This is not spiritual apathy, but rather a detachment from your own preferences and plans in favor of doing what God wants above all else.[35] Self-knowledge is important to grow. Can you identify what obstacles are preventing you from being sincerely open to God's will? These might be attachment to your own will, to a person, to material things, to image or status, or even to long held attitudes or internal dispositions. Often times it's fears of various kinds that prevent us from moving forward. Letting go of attachments and renouncing fears creates a freedom to be open to God's perfect plan.

After clarifying your thinking and pondering your internal indifference, fears must be dealt with. The most predominant fears which can paralyze discernment will be addressed next.

---

35 "We ought not to seek health rather than sickness, wealth rather than poverty, honor rather than dishonor, a long life rather than a short one," says St. Ignatius of Loyola in "Principle and Foundation" in the beginning of the *Spiritual Exercises*.

Chapter Six

Overcoming Fears

For those who experience immediate joy and even elation at the idea of a call to religious life, it is not uncommon for fears to emerge later. This was Sr. Veronica's experience:

> I did not experience any immediate fears concerning my call to religious life, but later, these did come. Over the next months and years leading up to my entrance into the convent, many fears arose in my heart. A primary concern for me was the question of living a life of celibacy. I had always pictured myself married with children, and I had serious doubts that I could actually be happy or fulfilled living a celibate life. Would God really be enough to satisfy my heart? Could I actually be happy without a husband or children of my own? Other fears included loneliness, a loveless life, that my gifts would be wasted, and that I would be bored, particularly with prayer.

Sr. Veronica's fears are experienced by many, if not most women discerning religious life. Others include: fear of unworthiness; fear of failure; fear of commitment; fear of the permanence of the vocation; fear of letting go of family, friends, and other attachments; and a fear of getting discernment wrong, among others. At the beginning of your discernment journey, you may not be able to articulate your fears or questions. But if you try to consider your fears and to put names to them, you will be able to address them head on. This process is very valuable; if you can turn your vague, gnawing fears into real questions, then finding answers to your questions will be the process by which you have dispelled your worries!

Let's look at these common fears one by one.

Fear of never gaining certainty about being called

There are times in the discernment process that feel cloudy and dark, and there are times of sunshine and light. It is important to keep in mind that God wants you to know your vocation more than you want to know it. God is the initiator. This is a gift He is offering you. No one wants you to open the gift more than He does. If you are taking steps toward Him, He will run out to meet you! He is not going to leave you wandering in the desert of endless discernment! The important part is actively taking steps toward Him. Keep moving forward! If you ask Him for the grace of clarity in your discernment, you will receive it.

Fear of loneliness

We are made for communion. This reality goes to the very core of our being and motivates our desires and decisions. This is because we are made in the image and likeness of God, Who is an unending giving and receiving of selfless love. We are already hungering to be part of this divine exchange here and now. That is what Pope John Paul II spent his whole pontificate trying to teach us: the meaning of our life is found in learning to make a sincere gift of self in love. If I do not learn to make a sincere gift of myself in love, I will live an unfulfilled life. If I am married and do not learn to live what John Paul II called "the law of the gift,"[36] I will be lonely even in marriage. If I am a religious and I do not learn this, likewise, I will be lonely. I have an equal chance of living a lonely and unfulfilled life in any vocation. Naturally, the opposite is also true. Loneliness does not have to do with a state of life; loneliness, in part, has to do with how we live our vocation.

There are different aspects of communion in religious life, just as there are different aspects of communion in marriage. A wife experiences a certain fulfillment from being loved, cherished, and served by her husband and by loving, cherishing, and serving him. She experiences a different kind of fulfillment in welcoming a child, protecting, nurturing,

---

36   St. John Paul II, in his Wednesday audiences, gave a teaching which has become known as the *Theology of the Body* in which he develops the concept of the gift of self being necessary for finding meaning and fulfillment in life. This teaching can also be found in the documents of the Second Vatican Council, particularly *Gaudeum et Spes*.

teaching, and forming this child. Both forms of communion are experiences of self-giving love, love given and love received. So too, in religious life there are different aspects of communion. There is the communion with God which is experienced directly through prayer. But this is incomplete. In this life, the religious will never be entirely complete, done with the yearning, searching, and the longing to be filled. The consummation of our marriage to God is scheduled post-mortem. Only in heaven will the search be over and the longing fulfilled.

Even so, the taste of heaven we receive now is enough to keep us on the journey. In addition to the direct communion with God that a religious experiences through prayer, there is the communion she experiences with her sisters in community, and this can be a great consolation. Religious life is an intensely relational environment. As a religious, you enter into a communion of persons who have each been called by God to share together in this way of life. The degree that you enter into the available communion is the degree that you will be fulfilled here and now. It is in relationship to your sisters in community that your love of God can be expressed, made tangible and real. A married woman can say, "I love you," but then she must show those words to be true through her actions, perhaps by giving her husband her full attention and affection when he comes home from work, or perhaps by giving him space! She will show her love by recognizing his unique goodness and the sacrifices he makes for her and the children, and she will find ways to affirm these gifts in him (sometimes with words and sometimes without). She will find acts of service to communicate her love, perhaps by preparing his favorite dinner, picking up his socks with joy, and in a thousand other creative ways.

A religious sister has the opportunity to demonstrate her love for God firstly by loving and serving the sisters she lives with, by listening to them attentively when they want to talk, by helping them carry their burdens, by not judging them for their weaknesses, and by sharing herself with them (which can easily be overlooked as a form of loving another).

The next tier of love for a religious sister is the love expressed to those in her care, those that God has given her to love on His behalf. In the case of the community to which I belong, we enter into communion with God through evangelization and loving service to the poor. Religious sisters who teach show their love of God through instructing their students. Nursing sisters show their love of God by caring for the sick. As St. John reminds us, "No one has ever seen God; yet if we love one another, God remains in us, and His love is brought to perfection in us" (1 John 4:12).

And so in a religious life lived well, there need not be a fear of loneliness. It likely will come, but no more or less than it will come to anyone else. If and when a religious is faced with loneliness, despite her best efforts to live faithfully, the important thing is *how* she responds to it. She must return to the mysterious truth that Jesus is alive in her, living His life in her. This is an implication of the mystery of the Incarnation. For an unfathomable reason, Jesus is pleased to dwell within her. He is pleased to experience loneliness again in her, and her loneliness lived in union with Him becomes a participation in the divine suffering that saves.

Fear of a loveless life

I had the experience once of a total stranger approaching me with the opening line, "You mean to tell me you don't have sex?" (This was in the Bronx, New York, where people may be a bit more forthright than in other parts of the country.) It is nothing less than shocking to many people when they discover that there are people in the world who freely choose a celibate life. Our choice is puzzling to many in our culture, which confuses sex with love, or perhaps, having given up on authentic love, has settled for sex as a substitute. It could seem on the surface, to some, like choosing a loveless life. Nothing could be further from the truth! In fact, our life says to the world, "There is such a thing as love—real, eternal, undying love!"

Celibacy is meant to increase our capacity for love, not diminish it! But it is worth looking at the fear of freely giving up the marital expression of love. Our natural and God-given sexual drive is good. It is part of us, and it is there for a reason. It is not, however, the central driving principle of the human person. It would be more accurate to say that *love* is the central driving principle of the human person. We are made to know and to be known, to love and to be loved, for eternal communion. Ultimately, we are made for a virginal communion of love which transcends the marital embrace.

When discerning a religious vocation, it is very important to look squarely at the sacrifices entailed and not diminish the renunciation required. You'll have to face it at some point. It is best to face it before you enter. Even so, you will confront this sacrifice again and again. The self-denial is not once chosen and forever forgotten. No, we take up our cross daily and follow Jesus. This sacrifice will be keenly felt. As women, many of us grew up planning our wedding, our honeymoon, and our dream house. We had our first three children named before we graduated! We are internally wired for the intimacy of marriage and child-bearing. So if God is calling us to something different, we will have to learn to offer those unfulfilled desires to God as an offering and a profound act of worship.

The deep desire for spousal union however, does not go unfulfilled; the fulfillment is found in God alone. The virgin is allowing herself to be pursued and captivated by God Himself, and a new bond of consecration is a covenant bond to be brought to its apex in heaven.

Religious life does not require you live a loveless life! The contrary is true! The religious has been sought after by Love Himself! You could say that the religious life requires you to live a *love-filled* life. But it takes a different form than the natural and beautiful course of marriage and family life. Your life as a religious need not be—and in fact, should not be—isolated, lonely, or loveless. Eucharistic devotion holds a privileged place for fostering growing intimacy between the religious and the Lord. And it makes sense that it should when you consider that the Eucharist is Jesus Christ physically and spiritually present, body, blood, soul, and divinity. In other words, He is really there as a man and as God.[37]

---

37   Reflecting on why religious may experience something less than fulfillment, Fathers Dominic Hoffman and Basil Cole surmise that "Failure to live close to Christ in the tabernacle may be a very significant, if not the main reason, we have missed fullness of heart." *Consecrated Life: Contribution of Vatican II* (St. Paul, 2005).

While the possibility exists to experience God in other ways, through the gift of contemplative union for example, the Eucharist we *always* have with us. God in His humility is perpetually there for us. Regardless of our moods, problems, and sins, we can be certain of both His love and His availability.

Fear of never being a mother

In addition to spousal fulfillment, women experience the need to give of self in another way—a concrete, tangible, and life-giving way. Here something can be said of spiritual motherhood. Motherhood is the key to the identity of every woman. Because religious sisters will not have children physically does not mean they will not experience motherhood—they do experience it, albeit in a different way! In natural motherhood, a woman welcomes and affirms the life of an eternal, unique, unrepeatable person. She devotes herself, body and soul, to the nurture, care, protection, and well-being of the new person in her womb. Spiritual motherhood can be seen as welcoming and affirming the life of an eternal, unique, and unrepeatable person, and while not carried in the womb, certainly carried in the heart. Furthermore, it is devoting body and soul to the nurture, care, protection, and eternal wellbeing of this other person and all other persons, for God's sake. "Consecrated women are called in a very special way to be *signs of God's tender love for the human race*."[38]

First, it is by means of their consecration and life of

---

38   *Vita Consecrata*, 57 (emphasis in the original).

prayer that religious women exercise their spiritual motherhood. The vocation is not for herself alone; it is inherently *for others.* When "she makes those vows she makes them for her children."[39] Prayer of intercession and a life of sacrifice are powerful hidden means of mothering souls unto life eternal.

Sisters begin to experience the gift of their own maternity blooming within them in a variety of simple ways. Sr. Ann Kateri experiences it through some of the poor who come regularly to the door, but also through serving the sisters under her care. "Mateo[40] comes to our door every day for a sandwich and hot chocolate. He's in his mid-40s but he has the mental capacity of a six-year-old, and although his repeated doorbell ringing can become annoying, his smiles and simple request for a Mickey Mouse cake for his birthday bring such joy to my heart." Spiritual children draw love out of the religious sister's maternal heart. God allows people to come into our lives in order to provoke care, concern, and selflessness from us, to expand our capacity to love.

Shortly after her final profession of vows, Sr. Mary Emmanuel had a very vivid experience of her spiritual motherhood. Martin, a man from the Indian Reservation in California where her community served, had turned his life around and was about to graduate from his training course to become a Marine. She was asked by her superiors if she would

---

39   Mother Revelation says these words referring to the mystery of spiritual motherhood in the film *For Love Alone* (CMSWR). I highly recommend that you watch this short film, available through Amazon and iTunes.

40   The names of people associated with the sisters through the apostolate have been changed to protect the individuals' privacy.

travel to California and be present as a moral support for his graduation. Martin was overcome with tears of joy on this milestone day to have "family" in the audience when he expected to have none. He proceeded to introduce the habited and veiled Sr. Mary Emmanuel to all his friends as "Mom"! And what's more, on the flight back to the reservation, when Martin was moved to first class because of his military uniform, he asked if his "mom" could be moved up too! The obliging flight attendant was no doubt surprised to have a nun and a marine as mother-son duo in first class! Sr. Mary Emmanuel's experience with Martin highlights the need that every human person has to be mothered. In this case it came in the simple form of being there—simply being present.

The experience of mothering souls is as vast and varied as human life. For Sr. Kelly Francis, the experience of spiritual motherhood is beginning to be felt. So far in her young religious life, it has been most keenly felt in simple and ordinary tasks of service like tying a child's shoe, placing a bag of groceries in an older lady's cart, or clearing away someone's place setting at the soup kitchen. These are the things that all mothers do dozens of times a day—simple acts of loving service done because God is present in His children, and He is worthy to be served. Providing the spiritual formation that is quite naturally expected from religious sisters has also been an experience of spiritual motherhood for Sr. Kelly Francis. The simple task of listening to people, teaching children to pray, and being available has been quite profound and life-giving for this young sister.

Growing in the understanding of the gift of celibacy and its implications takes time. At first, celibacy can be felt

Fear of an unhappy life

Are religious sisters really happy—deep down, even without a husband and children? This is a question which every religious sister most likely asked at some point during her discernment. The attraction to marriage and family life, to becoming a wife and a mother, is usually strong, and at first glance it can seem that giving up something that you desire so deeply would lead to unhappiness. However, if happiness is achieved by learning to make a true, selfless gift to another, then you can be sure the possibility of happiness awaits you within the religious life just as in it does in marriage. As Pope Benedict XVI said so movingly at World Youth Day in Cologne: "Dear young people, the happiness you are seeking, the happiness you have the right to enjoy, has a name and a face: It is Jesus of Nazareth, hidden in the Eucharist. Only He gives the fullness of Life to humanity! With Mary, say your own 'Yes' to God, for He wishes to give Himself to you."

Fear of boredom

If you want to see a sister really laugh, tell her that one of your fears about entering religious life is being consigned to life of monotony and boredom. The life of a religious sister is so full that there is never even a moment of boredom! But the fear is often more specifically about boredom in prayer, or rather a feeling of inadequacy to measure up to expectations. With so many hours of prayer each day, how will I be able to stand the silence? How will I learn to pray? You will learn to pray by praying. You will learn the life by living it. Religious life is an adventure. First of all, you are growing in loving intimacy with the God who is infinite. Secondly, you are living in community with sisters from many different backgrounds and experiences. Thirdly, you are learning and experiencing new things on a daily basis. Take my word for it, religious life is many things, but it is not boring!

But let's just speculate that it *is* boring for some, or that during certain seasons of life it could be monotonous. At these times we remember the rhythm and routine that the whole universe obeys. The sun rises every morning and sets every evening, without wavering, without fail. Whoever looked at a sunrise as monotonous or stifling in its regularity?

Fear of unworthiness

When you think about the reality of being called and chosen by God, the possibility that it's specifically and personally *you* that He wants seems impossible, unreal. How could it be? You know yourself enough to know you're no saint. It's easy to think that it must all be some mistake.

This is the oldest trick in the book. Your ancient enemy tells you that you are not good enough, that you're unworthy of such a lofty calling. By believing this lie, you belittle God's mercy and His power to save. The truth is you *aren't* worthy. None of us is worthy. We are sinful creatures and beggars before God. But He chooses whomever He wants. The prerogative is His. But we must also remember that we are His beloved and that one word from His lips can heal us. As we pray at every Mass, "Lord, I am not worthy that you should enter under my roof, but only say the word and my soul shall be healed." Do not get trapped in the unworthiness web. Simply pray that the God who loves you and is calling you will make you worthy. Leave it all up to Him.

Sometimes the roots of feelings of unworthiness have to do with your past history. As you start to move seriously toward a religious vocation, all kinds of memories of past sins and failures replay in your mind to accuse you all over again. If these things have been brought to Confession, it is important to remember that the loving forgiveness and mercy of God has not expired! Remind yourself of the truth and try not to give in to the lies of the accuser who would have you believe that you are unforgivable or incapable of living out a religious vocation. Of course, it is important to have had a true and sincere conversion from the past life of sin and to have lived a virtuous life for an extended period of time in the world before attempting to enter religious life. The best test of capacity for religious life is the ability to live a solid, prayerful, virtuous life of discipleship in your own environment before making the big step into the convent.

Fear of failure

Closely related to the fear of unworthiness is the fear of failure. There can be different roots for this fear, but one likely root may be your ideas about the vocation. If your image of religious life is overly idealistic, then fear of failure will be a natural consequence. If your image of the sisters has you feeling awed, you could easily be intimidated and unable to imagine yourself in their ranks. When you realize that every one of the sisters, even the most venerable, are human beings with weaknesses and sins of their own, your fear of failure will diminish.

Furthermore, the fear of failure indicates too much

reliance on self. "Cast your cares upon Jesus because He cares for you," teaches St. Peter. Self-reliance is the enemy of a religious vocation. Actually, it is the enemy of the Christian life. If you begin to trust more in God and less in yourself, God will lead you. This applies to your prayer life—and everything else.

Fear of permanence

It is important to remember that entering the convent and making final vows is not the same thing! There is a long journey to be made from crossing the threshold of the convent to lying prostrate[41] before the altar at perpetual profession. Approximately seven years separate the two events!

However, it seems that people in this generation are marrying at a later age and other lifelong commitments are being delayed. There seems to be a fear of permanence. Perhaps it's the desire to keep our options open and a fear of being trapped. Having seen the divorce rate rise so significantly over the last two generations has likely created a fear of getting into a permanent commitment and then having it not work out. Perhaps the idea of a lifelong *anything* is beginning to feel more and more unreal and unattainable.

This is where trust and a sense of risk are needed. First, we return again to that touchstone of our discernment: It is a loving Father in Whom you are placing your trust, not in yourself and not in a statistic. Trust Him. If God is leading

---

41   The liturgical gesture of lying prostrate during perpetual profession of vows, as during ordination, symbolizes the total gift of the person who is quite literally laying down her life.

you, what have you to fear? Even if the "fresh and green pastures" turn into the "valley of darkness," don't you want to be following Him? Wouldn't you rather be *with* Jesus in the valley of darkness than *without* Him... anywhere? Risk is so essential. You will never have all the data or all the answers. You will never know the outcomes in advance—not for your vocation and not for any decision you will make in life. At a certain point, you must gather up your courage and make a leap of faith. And consider this: it is *only* in making the leap that you will discover the graces and blessings in the opportunities that await you there.

Fear of leaving your family

This fear will have to be faced by all who intend to grow up, mature, and live adult Christian lives. No matter what you do in life, a certain amount of letting go of your family will be required of you. If you were to get married and start a family, your relationship with your mom and dad would necessarily change. "That is why a man leaves his father and mother and clings to his wife" (Genesis 2:24). At the end of a talk on religious life, one of the first questions usually asked is, "Do you get to go home and visit your family?" And the answer is yes, we get to go home every year, and this is true of many religious communities.[42] But the question implies that the religious life requires a sacrifice that is surprisingly unique, when in fact those called to marriage have plenty of

---

42 Customs regarding home visits vary from community to community, but I don't know of an active religious community that does not allow for a periodic home visit.

sacrifices to make too, as all disciples of Christ do. Who's to say you would have gotten married and lived next door to your parents? Imagine getting engaged and saying to your fiancé, "I am so happy about your wonderful job opportunity in New York, but if we're not going to get back to Ohio for a couple of weeks every year, I don't know if I can marry you." Ridiculous, isn't it? Your vocation necessarily takes you from the maternal apron-strings to the mission field.

Imagine Jesus's departure from home when the time came for Him to find His cousin John, to be baptized, and to begin His work. He could have found such convincing reasons not to go! Who was going to take care of His mother as she aged? How would she take care of herself as a widow with no other children? Didn't He have a responsibility to at least stay close to home? And think of how easily Mary could have clung to Him and not let Him go. We can imagine it because that's the way we tend to be, but it is unthinkable to project our dispositions on the perfections of Mary, who when the time came, did let her Son go; in fact, she so fully supported Him in His mission of redemption that we now call her co-redemptrix. Doing the Father's will was the food that sustained Jesus and Mary both. They were of one heart and one mind. "Be it done unto me according to the Father's will" could easily have been the motto of the Holy Family.

As necessary and as inevitable as letting go of family is, it is difficult. God's grace is with you. If you pray for the courage and the strength, you will certainly receive it.

Fear of letting go

The fear of letting go is a catch-all for all the myriad

of fears that have not been specifically addressed. This category also includes letting go of friends and hobbies, material things, forms of entertainment, and independence. This is particularly difficult in our American culture which prizes independence so highly. Letting go of control is a process that develops over time, as you learn to be docile and interdependent within a religious community. The prerequisites are willingness, humility, and always a sense of humor.

In order to say yes to one thing, you will have to say no to other things. Recently I was helping with a vocation workshop with a Dominican sister (of the Dominican Sisters of St. Cecilia) at a Catholic high school in Texas. I was moved by her story. Early on in her discernment, she was living for a time in Europe with good friends who were newly married. And as the weeks went on, she began to observe her friend declining many things she once enjoyed, a glass of wine at dinner, a ski weekend, and other things. As she said no, she did it with a twinkle in her eye and an unmistakable joy. It was growing obvious that her friend had a very good reason to be declining these good things—the reason was the new life which she carried within. How easy it was to say no to these trifles in comparison to the yes that she was saying to a new person who was destined to live eternally and who had been entrusted to her. So it is with all vocations. Your vocation is so precious you *want* to reject anything that threatens it.

But the fact is, sometimes joy can be slow in coming. Often there are many tears in the separations, departures, and renunciations which are necessary before embracing religious life. More than one sister has cried all the way to the convent! As one mother of a sister reflected, "If it were easy, there would be a lot more people doing it."

Fear of discerning to enter and then later discovering that I was wrong

Many women express a fear of not getting it right, of discerning to enter religious life only to leave later on. This fear is very understandable, especially if you have known of peers entering a community only to leave a few years later. The best antidote to this fear is the foundational virtue of trusting in the God Who loves you. If you engage in an intentional discernment process which is guided by prayer and a spiritual director, and you are doing all you can to discover and follow God's will, be sure you will be blessed, no matter what happens. You can never be guaranteed of knowing all ends. Life was never meant to be that way. We do our best, we take risks, and we live life, leaving plenty of room for trusting and depending on God.

The choice for the religious life must be a free one. No matter how intentional and complete the discernment process was prior to entering, every sister should be encouraged to continue to discern more deeply at every step. Is this what God wants? Is this what I want? Can I do this? Often, profession of final vows doesn't come until seven or more years in the community. That gives you plenty of time to be certain.

"Do not be afraid because great courage is required if we are to open the doors to Christ, if we are to let Christ enter into our hearts... Do not be afraid! If you begin to lose courage, turn to Mary, seat of wisdom; with her at your side, you will never be afraid."

~St. John Paul II

Chapter Seven

The Six-Month Discernment Challenge

Looking back at the agony of my own discernment, I can see that what would have helped me was a *plan for discernment*, a clear idea of how to arrive at a decision. Once you feel the initial stirrings of a call and it grows more difficult to dismiss the possibility of religious life, and your heart is genuinely opening to the possibility of a call, your restlessness should lead you to action.

The first thing to know is that *time is needed*. It takes time to discern well because it takes time to listen well and pray well. It takes time to allow your questions to be answered and for clarity to emerge. The goal is to move from discernment to decision. You may consider setting aside some time dedicated to exploring the possibility of religious life through prayer and other means. I recommend taking the "sixth-month discernment challenge." By setting aside a fixed amount of time, you are not putting a time limit on God; rather it is so that you can fully enter into a more intensive time of prayer and action to figure out if this is the right direction for your life. You can always lengthen the six months, but I don't recommend shortening it.

Step One: Make a Commitment

The first step is making a commitment to the six-month discernment challenge. This is not to be taken for granted. It is important that the idea of setting aside time to intentionally discern is backed up by a commitment. Decide to do it and then tell one or two people of your decision so that they can hold you accountable. A spiritual director is a logical person to tell, if you have one already. (We will talk more about spiritual direction ahead in step three.)

You also may want to get a notebook and start a discernment journal. Many people benefit from keeping a journal during their discernment journey and beyond. Keeping a journal is important for many reasons. Firstly, it helps you to articulate what you are experiencing. This serves as a record of your spiritual experience and a great tool to prepare for meeting with a spiritual director. Also, as you record the ups and downs of your experiences, it helps you identify patterns and gives you an easy way to remember graces received. Your first journal entry can be a statement of your intention to enter wholeheartedly into the "six-month discernment challenge," point by point.

Step Two: Develop Your Prayer Life

During the "six-month discernment challenge," you will want to dedicate more time to prayer. As was mentioned in

faith that she decided to dedicate a year to God. It was her personal "Holy Year." Two things she was giving up during her year for God were smoking and cosmetics. No one told her to do this; she just felt compelled to change as she got closer to God.

As you grow you will notice obstacles to your new commitment to prayer, and you will now be ready to remove them. Some examples of possible obstacles are: too much Internet, TV, or other social media; overemphasis on material things; and certain types of music and films. Feeling the need to make certain changes is a natural and important consequence of growing in your spiritual life, because just as you learned in science class, two things cannot occupy the same space. Something, or rather Someone, is now taking up more space in your life and other things must give way.

You may find your daily patterns changing too. Perhaps you are being drawn to try to rise earlier and go to bed earlier so as to make time to pray. Perhaps you feel impelled to keep your room tidier because now you and Christ meet there more often. Love for Him impels you to do what were once mundane chores. Certain forms of entertainment are losing their attraction. Certain relationships suddenly do not seem helpful or consistent with your commitment to Christ. As your priorities shift, it is not uncommon to find yourself dressing differently and perhaps even making choices such as giving up certain friendships.

As you make real steps in following Christ, you will find your prayer deepening. As your prayer deepens and your habits change, *you* will change. So begins the adventure of transformation in Christ. Simple bread and wine are changed in their very substance in every Mass; we, too, are meant to be substantially changed daily through our contact with the Lord. As you experience prayer and virtue expanding in you, a need for guidance will likely be felt.

Step Three: Spiritual Accompaniment

Sr. Veronica was nineteen when she wrote her first letter of inquiry to the convent. Here was a sophomore college student, a bright and beautiful girl with a wonderful family and a seemingly endless litany of gifts and talents. She had the whole world before her, and she was ready to leave everything behind and enter the convent right away before she even graduated from her teens! She was not anguished by her possible call, but delighted at the possibility. But even at nineteen years old, Sr. Veronica had the good sense to know that she needed to be accompanied along the way. She needed guidance, someone to talk with, and to help her work through her fears.

Your vocation is an intensely personal thing. It is the revelation of your identity spoken from the Father's heart to yours. But this adventure of discovery, personal as it is, is not made well unaccompanied. Man was not made to be alone. This truth has many implications. It is a very good idea to find a spiritual director to meet with on a regular basis as you discern. A spiritual director can be a priest, a religious, or even a lay person. You will want to find someone who is living their faith, someone who is further along the path of holiness and wisdom than you are, someone who is trained in spiritual direction, and someone whom you trust.

This is a tall order, and there seems to be a shortage of

available spiritual directors. Our priests tend to have more work than any one person can reasonably handle, and so it is understandable when requests for spiritual direction go unmet. However, if you tell your priest that you are discerning religious life and would just like to meet with him for the next six months, it is more likely that he could find time for this, knowing that he's not committing to a life-long spiritual direction relationship. Or, he may be able to recommend someone in the parish who does spiritual direction.

Another possible solution is connecting with the vocation director of the community you are most interested in; most vocation directors would be open to speaking with you on a monthly basis in order to answer your questions and help you sort out your inner-life.

It is important that the person accompanying you understands discernment and religious life. It is very difficult to make a good discernment without the help of a guide. We were never meant to journey alone in life.[47]

Step Four: Don't Date and Discern

During the "six-month discernment challenge," consider not dating. Dating is ultimately for the purpose of discerning

---

47   The longstanding tradition of seeking spiritual direction was affirmed by Pope Benedict XVI in the context of a General Audience: "I would like to add that the invitation to have recourse to a good spiritual father who can guide every individual to profound knowledge of himself and lead him to union with the Lord so that his life may be in ever closer conformity with the Gospel still applies for all priests, consecrated persons, and lay people, especially the youth. To go towards to the Lord, we always need a guide, a dialogue. We cannot do it with our thoughts alone. And this is also the meaning of the ecclesiality of our faith, of finding this guide." (Sep 16, 2009).

marriage. If you are currently dating, then date! Enjoy it. Have fun. Maybe even consider entering into a prayerful, guided, discernment of the sacrament of marriage. This is a noble and important undertaking. Would that all marriages were preceded by thoughtful and prayerful discernment! However, if you are feeling restlessness within, and you don't feel you will have peace until you take adequate time to seriously discern religious life, then decide not to date at the same time as discerning religious life. It will only be a source of needless drama and perhaps a broken heart.

In my experience of suggesting this moratorium on dating, an immediate fear arises for many young women: What if I take six months (or a year) to discern religious life and that's precisely when my would-be, future husband comes along and I miss him? This is a matter of trust. Let go of the controls. Will you trust the God Who made you and Who loves you? Will you trust that He wants you to discover your vocation more than you want to discover it? This is the truth. He has a dream for you and this dream is His gift to you. Trust Him. He is worthy of it.

Not that this is an easy thing. Sr. Veronica describes her struggle to let go:

> In the depths of my heart there was always a question, "Could I really be happy if I didn't get married?" I would beg the Lord to let the call pass me by and simply to allow me to live a "normal life" with a husband and children. Because I was attending a good Catholic university I felt that any of the men there could be a potentially good choice for a husband. Daily I would ask

the Lord, "What about him?" or "What about that one?" and each time the answer would come back to me, "It won't be enough for you; he won't be enough for you. There is more. I have made you for more." And I would internally argue back with the Lord, "Oh yes it would be enough, I promise you it would." And the Lord would respond, "No, your heart was made for more. The married life won't be enough for you." Over those years, I went out on a couple of dates, hoping a spark would fly in my own heart, but nothing did. I didn't want to marry just anyone. I wanted God's will alone.

We are so often more than ready to settle for less than what God wants.

Step Five: Pick a Few Communities and Start Visiting

The next point in your plan for discernment is to narrow down the field. You can't discern every community, just like you can't date every boy! The last thing you want to do is get out the phone book and begin calling all the religious communities, starting with the A's! Instead, look first to the communities that God has allowed to cross your path, the sisters who teach in your school or work in your campus ministry. It's always a good principle to begin with what is right before you. If you find that you're not attracted to the sisters in your closest circles, or perhaps there are no sisters in your immediate community, then the Internet is a great way to find out what communities are out there. As you view the communities, select a few whom you find attractive, and start there.[48]

Once you have two or three communities picked out, it's now time to gather up your courage and make a phone call. You are probably more comfortable with texting, or you would rather email. Those steps are fine, but there is nothing like hearing a voice of a sister on the other end of the line who is warm and friendly and is happy to give you her time. I've been on the receiving end of countless first-time vocation calls, so I realize this is not an easy step. You won't be the first to hang up once or twice before you get the nerve to say something to the mysterious sister on the phone line! Your discernment is like a dance. God is leading, but your feet have to follow His. It is important to make a step forward for the continued revelation of His will.

See how the first call goes, and walk through the doors as they open. If the vocation director invites you to visit, take another step and schedule a "come and see." On a "come and see" you'll have the opportunity to get a feel for the sisters' daily schedule. You will wake up when they do and move through the day with them. You will experience the way they pray, the way they live, what their relationships are like, and what their work entails.

For Sr. Chiara the "come and see" visit was critically important in dispelling preconceived ideas. After merely seeing a newsletter of the community, she quickly concluded that this community was not the one for her. However, on

---

48   A directory of religious communities can be found at www.cmswr.org. "Come and see" retreats are posted and updated on this page as well.

her first visit she described herself as being on "cloud nine" and every single detail of her first "come and see" seemed to have seared a deep impression on her. To this day, she can recount it in exquisite detail!

What can you expect on a "come and see" visit? This is a chance to be in the convent and to experience the life from the inside. Most communities call these visits "come and sees" because these are the very words Jesus Himself used when a couple of disciples asked Him awkwardly, "Where do you stay?" Naturally, Jesus knew that their question was deeper than wanting to know His street address, so He extended an initiation for them to come and see for themselves (John 1:39-41). He offers them an opportunity to get all their questions answered at once because He offers them an opportunity to *be* with Him.

Good advice to follow on a "come and see" is simply to go with the flow. Do what the sisters do and try to fit in. Be observant not only of the sisters, but also pay attention to your own inner reactions to the experience. Even though it sounds counterintuitive, try to set aside the discernment question while with the sisters. Try to "turn off" the analysis in favor of simply *living the experience.* If you can manage to be present to the moment and enjoy it, later, once you return home, you will analyze your experience, focusing on what you did and how you felt. The reason this approach is helpful is because a person can easily get lost in her head—caught up in evaluating and comparing and therefore miss the grace of the moment!

Often communities will have a dress code for the discernment weekend. Our "come and see" dress code is a long, loose-fitting skirt and modest top (not low cut and not form fitting). Typically you will be expected to "unplug" while you are in the convent, meaning no phone, not even for texting or emails. (No, it is not appropriate to post a picture of your first convent dinner on Instagram!) You should plan on leaving your hair straightener and mascara at home. You won't need any jewelry or accessories either. Plan to keep it simple. (I had all these things on my first "come and see," except for the straightener. I did bring a blow-dryer and no fewer than four pair of shoes.)

Fr. Benedict Groeschel often entertained us with stories of His own discernment path, including the story of his first "come and see." He blamed the friary cuisine as being the cause of his own rerouting from the Capuchins in the New Jersey province to the Capuchins in the New York province. As the story goes, Fr. Benedict was sixteen years old and long aware of his vocation to the priesthood. Furthermore, he had already made the decision that the Capuchins were the order for him. "The Capuchins... were like some unseen star that exerted a powerful gravitational pull on me. I believed it was simply my destiny to enter their orbit."[49] And the next step was to make his first visit to the friary. He was mesmerized by the friar who opened the door, specifically by his beard, his habit, the cord around his waist, and his rosary. He was exactly like the image from the books Fr. Benedict had read. How utterly like all the holy cards this friar looked! Once inside, Fr. Benedict was taking in every detail of everything

---

49   John Collins, *A Friars Tale: Remembering Fr. Benedict Groeschel, CFR* (Our Sunday Visitor), 47-49.

that's why no man ever impressed me... and the litany went on." Sr. Ana Chiara was able to make sense of herself only in light of her vocation.

Confirmation of your discernment conclusion comes also from the trusted guides who have been accompanying you along the way, your spiritual director and your vocation director. These are people you trust and who have been getting to know you deeply. They will offer valuable insight into the will of God as it unfolds toward a decision. It is important to remember that the community is discerning the will of God just as you are. They are asking, "Lord, are You sending us this woman? Is she called here? Will she grow in holiness and become the saint she is meant to be by living this charism with us?" Perhaps the vocation director will ask you to take certain steps before entering or going further in your relationship with the community. Take this guidance seriously. She is trying to help you.

Affirmation of your call may come from close friends and maybe even family. Don't be surprised if you start to feel like you are the last one to know about your own vocation! You may begin to hear many people say things like, "I knew this all along. I always suspected you would do something like this," or "I was wondering how long it was going to take you to figure this out; I've seen it coming for years!" This is deeply affirming when it happens, and you can consider this a confirmation of your vocation.

However, it is not true that if such confirmations from family and friends do *not* come, that you aren't being called. Parents have famously been resisting this way of life for centuries! It should be no surprise when parents resist their children's decisions. St. Francis and St. Clare suffered this to extremes. St. Francis was locked in the cellar dungeon of his home by his infuriated father, and St. Clare had to sneak out of her home in the middle of the night if there was to be any hope of escaping her family to follow in the footsteps of Francis. If you find yourself in conflict with parents who resist your vocation, know that you are in good company. The important thing is to honor your father and your mother and to follow Christ. Jesus knew we would face confrontations on this point and His teaching is clear: "If anyone prefers father or mother to me, he is not worthy of me" (Matt 10:37).

Looking for confirmations should not be equated with looking for signs. Sometimes people pray for signs and they do indeed receive what they ask for, and sometimes they don't. Signs are possible but they are neither necessary nor are they enough to confirm a call. For example, if you receive what you think is a sign, but have neither peace nor joy, nor do any doors open in your process of discernment, then the "sign" is questionable, if not entirely meaningless. A sign alone is not enough on which to base a life decision.

Sr. Mary Emmanuel had a first-hand experience of the danger in asking for signs: getting what you ask for! At twenty-three years old, while volunteering in Belize, Central America, she was looking forward to returning home after her year of service and marrying her long-term boyfriend. Unexpectedly, something began stirring within her and she suspected (and feared) that it was a call to the religious life. "I decided to ask the Lord for a sign," she explained. "I wasn't going to let go of this wonderful man unless I knew for certain that I was called." While she was walking back to the apartment she shared with four other women, a strange thing happened: the wind blew and a holy card landed on her foot! It was a nine-hour novena to the Infant of Prague. Sr. Mary Emmanuel thought a nine-hour novena preferable to a nine-day novena so she set out to get her sign.

On the ninth hour of her novena, after a long day of teaching, she returned to her apartment and plopped down on the hammock waiting for the sign she had been promised. Then there was a knock on the door. It was Kevin, her roommate's boyfriend. What did he come in to talk about? Religious life. "Have you been thinking about religious life?" He asked out of the clear blue. "Why did you ask that?" Sr. Mary Emmanuel inquired. "I don't know. I've just seen you praying a lot." Kevin then went on to share about his sister who was a religious sister and that she was the most joyful person he knew.

Sr. Mary Emmanuel received her answer—a sign, just as she had asked for. But to her mind, this was the wrong answer! She didn't want it to go this way! Stubbornly, she asked for another sign. The moral is: if you are not ready to receive the answer, don't ask the question. Pray first for an open heart because no sign will be enough for one whose heart is closed.

Step Seven: Take a Leap of Faith

Finally, as you find that your growing clarity has been confirmed by a deep sense of peace, by your spiritual director, and by the vocation director of the community, it is time to make the long-awaited step and begin the application process with a view toward entrance. The application process is straightforward but lengthy. It will include a thorough questionnaire with sections on your family, faith, education, work, ministry experience, and health. Most communities require a physical and a psychological evaluation. Usually a longer visit is required for applicants. This visit allows you the chance to once again test the call. It also allows the community to evaluate your readiness. How do you fit in? How do you adjust to the schedule, the prayer, the work and the relationships in community? Do you seem happy and thriving in community life? Does this seem to be a place where you can grow into the saint you were created to be? If you are invited to enter after the application process is complete, this in itself is a confirmation of your call.

Many women are surprised that the emotional roller coaster ride isn't necessarily over once they reach the long desired clarity about their call. All temptations don't evaporate when you finally come to a decision, and you likely will find new opportunities to say yes again. If you are applying to enter a religious community and are broadsided by a powerful attraction, this gives you the opportunity to freely choose Christ again in the face of another possibility. You could choose the crush, or you can choose Christ. Your freedom makes your love more authentic and more beautiful.

Do not be surprised if you experience cold feet, uncertainties and self-doubt. This is to be expected. Your thorough and well-thought-out discernment process will continue to support you. As doubts surface, you will be able to go back to the conversations, the prayer times, the peace, the confirmations that brought you to clarity to begin with. Take out your discernment journal and reread the graces that have marked your path and pray for the grace to "be not afraid." There are emotional ups and downs through this process and it can be expected that even after you make a firm decision to enter, you will continue to have ups and downs. Human life is just this way. You can be sure that the undulations will eventually settle down, and your tidal waves will become rolling waves, which will eventually give way to only occasional ripples.

Sr. Mary of Hope shared the following experiences of deep confirmation:

> My call was confirmed over and over again by the presence of deep peace, even when the step I was taking was painful. So many times at Mass, the readings would confirm the step I was taking. I remember clearly the readings on the Friday before I left for the convent. Jesus asked Peter, "Do you love me more than these?" He was asking me simultaneously, "Do you love me more than these?"

Other confirmations will come only after entering, after taking the step, living the life, and then experiencing growth in yourself. Sr. Chiara had this experience: "One way my call to be a sister was confirmed was by the simple fact that I was growing more and more into the person God made me to be. I was growing spiritually, emotionally... in every way. I loved living our life and could see that I could continue to grow here to, please God, become a saint!"

Perhaps you go through the "six-month discernment challenge" with plenty of prayer and guidance and appropriate action steps, but the doors are *not* opening in front of you. In fact, if you feel like you are hitting a brick wall, and your spiritual director agrees that you have put in adequate time, prayer, and appropriate steps, yet you can both see that the doors are not opening, do not be discouraged! You too have had a successful discernment process. When you ask a question, you must to be open to taking no for an answer. This is a proof of interior freedom. You can confidently close the question of religious life. Perhaps the Lord is leading you to another form of consecration, such as consecrated virginity or membership in a secular institute. Or perhaps you'll be led to dating and pursuing marriage.

The truth is, sometimes the road is very unpredictable, even though we would prefer a nice, neat process of discernment which resembles a math problem: your open heart plus the "six-month discernment challenge" equals entrance date in religious community. But sometimes there are more steps than we bargained for.

Such was the case for Erin. Zealous in her faith and eager to follow His lead, Erin had spent a significant amount of time discerning both religious life and the married vocation. After living at convent for a whole summer, then taking a close look at marriage with several faithful Catholic couples in her circles, she felt certain that the Lord was calling her to religious life. Her heart was at peace at the thought of making a step and entering. She quit her job, sold her house, and entered the convent with the intention of giving herself totally to the Lord as His spouse.

A year and a half later, when it was clear to Erin and to her community that it was not the Lord's will for her to remain in religious life, it could be tempting to question what went wrong in discernment. The fact is nothing went wrong. In prayer, with spiritual direction, with ample guidance and reflection, a decision was made, and by all measures, it was a good decision. Erin shared:

> For me, entering religious life was undoubtedly the most important thing I have done in my life. I knew it was God's will for me at the time. The fruit it bore, and continues to bear, is monumental. When I entered religious life, I thought joyfully to myself, "This is it. God led me here and I will pursue holiness through this vocation." While in the convent, my prayer life grew and deepened. The personal formation I received was foundational to who I am now. I learned to become more docile to God's will.

In Erin's case, her health began to deteriorate significantly when she entered the convent. This healthy, athletic young woman began to have symptoms which caused her to see many doctors and take seemingly endless medical tests, all while losing as much as forty-five pounds and being entirely unable to participate in the life of the community. Finally, it became clear to everyone that this could not continue. Erin peacefully returned home knowing that God was still to be trusted, as difficult as it was to do so. He was manifesting His will for her through the reality of the circumstances.

Erin can see clearly now that God used the time in the convent to prepare her for her true vocation. "I have no doubt in my mind that entering the convent was essential to my growth in holiness, and it was an essential part of God's plan for my life. God's ways are not our ways, and sometimes He has to make things explicitly clear for us—through sickness or some other major life event—in order for us to take notice."

She returned home, found doctors who were able help her, and after a needed surgery, she made a complete recovery. She met a wonderful Catholic man, married, and has three beautiful children. "I am without a doubt living God's will for my life through the vocation of marriage. He led me down a winding, bumpy road of discernment, leading me to the convent, out of the convent, and into the sacrament of marriage. My desire was simply to follow His promptings, and I knew if I was faithful to Him, He would reveal His plan for me eventually."

If your discernment of religious life results in a closed door, you will do well to continue on your journey as the Lord leads. Keep your discernment journal and refer back to it. It seems God either could be closing the door, or now is not the right time for you. Either way, you can be completely at peace with ending this chapter of your discernment and waiting on the Lord to lead you to the next chapter of your life with Him.

The Six-Month Discernment Challenge

1. **Make a Commitment.** Commit to The Six-Month Discernment Challenge. It takes time to discern well. Consider setting aside six months or even a year to focus explicitly on your vocational discernment.

2. **Develop Your Prayer Life.** Discernment flows out of your relationship with God, so commit to Holy Mass, frequent Confession, adoration, and personal prayer time, including silence, praying with the Scriptures, and Marian Consecration.

3. **Seek Accompaniment.** Don't make the journey alone. Find a good spiritual director.

4. **Don't Date and Discern.** Discern marriage and religious life separately. Let the discernment of each vocation have its time and place.

5. **Start Visiting.** Narrow down the search. Pick a few communities that you are attracted to, make contact, and schedule a visit. Visit sooner rather than later.

6. **Look for Confirmations of the Call.** As you grow in clarity about your call, your heart will provide confirmations in the form of peace and joy. The community, your spiritual director, and those who know you best will also be sources of confirmation.

7. **Take a Leap of Faith!** Discernment should lead to decision. Some things you can only know for sure by doing. At a certain point, you've got to go for it.

Chapter Eight

The Contemplative Life

S ooner or later in your journey of discernment the question of the contemplative life[50] is likely to arise. Feeling called to religious life, you may ask yourself whether you may be called to an active order or a contemplative order. This chapter will help you know how to proceed when you come to this fork in the road. Firstly, some explanations will help. What is the contemplative life? Aren't we all called to be contemplative? What is the cloister? How can you know if it is for you?

Every Christian is indeed called to live a contemplative life. One of the great fruits of the Second Vatican Council was the emphasis on the Universal Call to Holiness.[51] Every single person has the capacity for a profound relationship with God to the point of transforming union, or oneness

---

50   Contemplation has a variety of meanings in Catholic tradition. In regard to religious life, "contemplative" denotes the form of life devoted more intensively to prayer and contemplation than other forms.

51   The Vatican II document *Lumen Gentium*, Chapter V, is dedicated to the Universal Call to Holiness.

with God. All consecrated people[52] have a special obligation
to live a deeply prayerful or contemplative life because we
are called to a special, more literal imitation of Christ, if I
may put it that way.[53] That being said, among those called
and chosen for *consecrated life* some have the special call to
the *contemplative life*. The contemplative life refers to communities who live religious life with prayer as the primary
focus and are not engaged in an outside apostolate, or if so,
in a limited way.

Within this broad designation, I mean to include both
cloistered contemplatives, such as the Carmelites of which St.
Thérèse of Lisieux was a member, and also the *non-cloistered*
contemplatives, such as the Contemplative Sisters of Adoration and Reparation.[54] We will look briefly at both categories.

The Cloistered Contemplative Path

"Sister" and "nun" are used interchangeably by many
to describe religious women, even though all sisters are not
nuns. Religious women are accustomed to this blurring of
the lines, and in charity will not correct you if you make the
error! But there is a difference. "Nun" specifically denotes
women who are called to the monastic or cloistered life; that
is, religious life ordered entirely to contemplation such as

---

52   "The first and foremost duty of all religious is to be the contemplation
of divine things and assiduous union with God in prayer." Canon 663-1.

53   The consecrated person living the evangelical counsels is living the
life the Lord chose for Himself and that which His mother also embraced.
Lumen Gentium, Chapter VI, 46.

54   The Contemplative Sisters of Adoration and Reparation were founded
by Ven. Mother Marie Thérèse of the Heart of Jesus in Paris in 1848.

lived by Poor Clares, Discalced Carmelite, Dominican, Passionist, and Trappistine nuns. The monastic life is defined by the *Catechism of the Catholic Church* as the consecrated life marked by the public profession of religious vows of poverty, chastity and obedience, and by stable community life (in the monastery) with the celebration of the Liturgy of the Hours in choir.[55] Some nuns (Poor Clare Nuns and perhaps others) make a fourth vow of enclosure; that is, to live their lives within the confines of the monastery itself, "hidden with Christ in God" (Col.3:3). The tradition of the Liturgy of the Hours, or the Divine Office as it also called, is a choral recitation or chanting of the psalms which is the official prayer of the Church. It traces its roots all the way back to the ancient Jewish people who recited morning prayers and made the daily evening sacrifice. This is a way of sanctifying the day, or making a return of each part of the day back to God.

We can understand the vocation of the contemplative nun as a call to "cleave to God with mind and heart"[56] through the concrete means of solitude, silence, constant prayer, and willing penance. She holds an honored place in the Mystical Body of Christ, for she reveals the glory of the Church, and is a wellspring of heavenly graces for the world.[57] The hidden life of contemplation behind the monastery wall is "the

---

55   The consecrated life is treated in the *Catechism of the Catholic Church*, 914-933.

56   *Perfectae caritatis*, 5

57   Ibid, 7

highest expression of consecrated life."[58] Hidden as it is, it can easily be forgotten altogether, and certainly suffers misunderstanding and under-appreciation.

In the early Middle Ages, if a young woman began to feel the first stirrings of a call, her discernment would likely have centered around a local monastery of nuns living the sixth-century Benedictine Rule.[59] In this day and age, when a young woman first feels a call, if she has any familiarity at all with religious life, it is more likely with active life. Yet, God in His love and mercy continues to call women to contemplative life, this most radical expression of spousal love. By their continuous sacrifice of praise, He is pleased to lavish blessings upon the world.

Jesus Christ, the second person of the Holy Trinity, chose to be enclosed in the womb of the Virgin Mary. He chooses still to be enclosed in every tabernacle of the world, waiting silently for your visit and for mine. By choosing the cloister, nuns choose to be enclosed with Him. Giving up possessions but also "space," this form of self-offering allows them to enter even more fully into the Eucharistic mystery.[60] They are like the hidden power source for the Church and for the world. They remain enclosed, offering their lives as a sacrifice with Christ for humanity. If God is calling you to this form of religious life, follow the advice of St. John Paul II and "Be not afraid!" The Church needs you; the world needs you!

---

58   John Paul II, as quoted by Gambari in *Religious Life* (Cambridge Scholars Publishing), 182

59   St. Benedict (480-547) is considered the Father of Western Monasticism.

60   *Vita Consecrata*, 59.

The Contemplative Without Enclosure

Some nuns are dedicated to the intense prayer, reparation, and intercession of the cloistered contemplative, but they also maintain some apostolic work that involves more interaction and exposure to the world and thus these nuns are not bound by enclosure. Two examples are the contemplative branch of the Missionaries of Charity, founded by Mother Teresa in New York City in 1976, and the Sisters of Adoration and Reparation founded by Ven. Mother Marie Thérèse in 1848. Mother Marie Thérèse understood her call to contemplation without enclosure through the image of a bird in an open cage. The cage is a symbol of the heart of Jesus: the door is open, and the bird is completely free, but chooses to remain within the cage, within the heart of Jesus.[61]

Misconceptions and Stereotypes

The contemplative life bears its share of inaccurate stereotypes. The biggest misconception about monastic life, according to Sr. Marie Claudette, is "that every day is the same, monotonous, or even boring. In reality, we never know what each day will hold. It's always a new adventure."

According to Sr. Mary Cecilia, "The biggest misconception about monastic life is that it is for people who can't 'make

---

61   This image was provided for me by Sr. Máire of Saint Joseph, a sister of the congregation of sisters of Adoration and Reparation on the Falls Road in Belfast, Ireland.

it' in the world." As it says in *A Right to Be Merry*,[62] "the woman who would make an ideal wife and mother or businesswoman is the one who will succeed in the cloister."

When I asked Sr. Máire of Saint Joseph what were the biggest misconceptions about her life, she had three ready answers. Firstly, "That we are running away from reality or that it is a form of escapism." Secondly, "That we are old-fashioned, trying to hold on to a relic of the past." And thirdly, "That we are not in touch with the modern world."

Running away from reality is an impossibility that anyone who attempts it quickly realizes. Reality will be right there in the convent waiting for you when you arrive. If a woman does attempt to enter the convent out of an effort to "escape," either she will learn to confront and deal with the issues she is attempting to flee, or she will end up leaving.

The criticism of holding on to a relic of the past calls into the question the relevance of a life focused on prayer. Jesus Himself addressed this question of giving Him too much devotion. Recall once again the story from the Gospels of the woman with the alabaster flask of very expensive ointment. She broke the flask and poured the oil over Jesus' s head in a gesture of extravagant devotion, filled with the fragrance of the ointment. There were some who were indignant, saying, "Why this waste? For this ointment might have been sold for more than three hundred denarii, and given to the poor." And they reproached her. But Jesus said, "Let her be; why do

---

62   Mother Mary Francis, PCC, *A Right to Be Merry* (Ignatius Press). This excellent book takes the reader behind the walls of the cloister for an inside look at cloistered religious life.

experience. She developed a closeness to Our Lady and sought her intercession. "A small group of us teenagers began making a Holy Hour together each week, and each time I brought with me an image of Our Lady of Guadalupe to place at the foot of the tabernacle. I remember introducing the first joyful mystery of the rosary at one of these meetings and asking Our Lady to help me to say yes to God as she had done." Once in college, Sr. Marie Claudette quickly found Catholic friends, and together they nurtured their faith through daily Mass and regular prayer and retreats. All of this rich prayer and peer support was the tilling and fertilizing needed so that the seed planted could spring out of the soil at the appointed time, which happened to be her first visit to the monastery.

Often as the journey of discernment progresses, the question of contemplative life emerges. If you begin to feel an attraction, proceed by selecting one or two contemplative communities to start with and make contact. Certainly, searching the Internet is one way, rather like a blind-date approach. Seeking recommendations from your pastor and diocesan vocation director also may yield a few good leads. Then it is a matter of proceeding step by step, walking through doors as they open, and allowing closed doors to steer you elsewhere.

Sometimes it is naively assumed that only quiet introverts, meek and mild bookish types, are those who join the cloister, surely not the boisterous extroverts and headstrong leaders! One Poor Clare sister shared that her vocation came as a shock to her family and friends partly because of her "wild and rebellious" streak! Ask any contemplative sister, or better yet, visit the cloister to see for yourself the dynamic and diverse personalities therein!

Indicators that you might be called to cloistered life are first and foremost the attraction of your own heart. Sr. Mary Cecilia relayed the following discernment story: "One young woman wrote to us and said that a priest suggested that she enter the monastery, but that every time she thought about doing so she burst into tears. We replied that this was probably an indication she was not called to the monastic life." Perhaps it seems too simple, but your heart will know.

A Final Word

In his recent Apostolic letter to contemplative women, Pope Francis reaffirmed the irreplaceable value of contemplatives for the Church:

> Through intercessory prayer, you play a fundamental role in the life of the Church. You pray and intercede for our many brothers and sisters who are prisoners, migrants, refugees and victims of persecution. Your prayers of intercession embrace the many families experiencing difficulties, the unemployed, the poor, the sick, and those struggling with addiction, to mention just a few of the more urgent situations. You are like those who brought the paralytic to the Lord for healing. Through your prayer, night and day, you bring before God the lives of so many of our brothers and sisters who for various reasons cannot come to Him to experience His healing mercy, even as He patiently waits for them. By your

prayers, you can heal the wounds of many.[68]

With his vivid affirmation of the practical value of the call to the contemplative life, I hope you find the courage to say yes if this is the gift you are offered by the Lord.

---

68   Pope Francis, *Vultum Dei quaerere*, 16.

Chapter Nine

What to Look for in a Religious Community

"The community of believers was of one heart and mind, and no one claimed that any of his possessions was his own, but they had everything in common."

~Acts of the Apostles 4:32

I never actually made a list when I was discerning, but I knew what I wanted because I encountered it in person the first time I met members of our community. I was attracted by the warm approachability and lack of pretense that I sensed in each one I met. The sisters and the friars possessed an obvious joy and a childlike simplicity. They were holy, and they were normal.

It was 1993, and Pope John Paul II was on his way to World Youth Day in Denver. My college was organizing a sixteen-bus pilgrimage to Colorado, and the Franciscan Friars and Sisters of the Renewal, out of the Bronx, New York, were slated to join us as spiritual leaders for the journey. I have a clear memory of meeting "Father Brother Robert"[69] under the big red and white tent. He was surrounded by students, telling one funny tale after the other. I almost couldn't figure out what I was looking at in this jolly, gray-clad, only semi-mobile, fascinating person! Oddly enough, suddenly it wasn't as difficult to imagine myself as part of a community. Something about this rag-tag, merry band was able to bridge the gap between my world and the mysterious world of religious.

In addition to the personal attraction I felt to the sisters and friars, I also had a deep attraction to Eucharistic adoration and to authentic Marian devotion (as exemplified in the faithful praying of the rosary and Marian consecration, among other things). These, too, would have been on the list, if there had been one. I was also attracted to the idea of serving the inner-city poor. I say "idea" because I had almost no experience of this yet, except through books. Evangelizing was something I did have a little experience with. (Remember, it was at a non-denominational youth group where I first started to hear the call.) These attractions were forming a semi-conscious "dream-list" of hopes for the community I would someday join (*if* I was called, that is!).

It is worth adding that I was also looking for a community who lived together in a convent and wore a religious habit. I could conceive of no other radical, visibly

---

69   Fr. Robert Stanion (1947-2012) was one of the original eight friars to begin the Franciscan Friars of the Renewal. He was a lay brother for many years before he went to seminary and was ordained a priest. He retained such a love for the vocation of lay brotherhood that he was known as "Father Brother" all his days, a nickname he loved!

counter-cultural way to live out the call to belong totally to Jesus as a religious sister. This attraction was not a response to an intellectual knowledge of religious life; it was simply an instinctive attraction.

It is important for you to realize as you discern that the Church does offer a definition of religious life. You need not be guided by your subjective notions alone. The Catechism of the Catholic Church, canon law, and other magisterial teachings provide us with a clear definition and description of the necessary characteristics of religious life. In 1983, St. John Paul II promulgated the *Essential Elements*,[70] which articulate what is vital for religious, based on the code of canon law. These nine elements are what make the religious life distinct.[71] They serve as a good guide as you explore various communities.

The nine essential elements of religious life are:

1. Consecration by public vows

2. Visible and stable community life

3. Evangelical mission

4. Prayer (communal, liturgical, and personal)

5. Asceticism

6. Public witness

---

70   *Essential Elements in the Church's Teaching on Religious Life as Applied to Institutes Dedicated to Works of the Apostolate* (Sacred Congregation for Religious and Secular Institutes)

71   It is important to realize that there are other forms of consecrated life. The items listed here are vital to the life of religious men and women, but consecrated virgins, hermits, and members of secular institutes are not characterized by all of these same elements.

7. Relation to the Church

8. Formation throughout life

9. Government based on faith

The document ends with an explanation of Our Lady as the perfect model for religious. Beyond what attracts me or you to a community, the Church provides objective guidelines. We will take a brief look at each of the essential elements in simple terms—by no means a thorough treatment, but an introduction.

Consecration by Public Vows

This first essential element is the foundation stone upon which the whole religious life is built. Let's take a look at all three key words: consecration, public, and vows. Chalices and churches and altars are consecrated, that is, set apart for a special, holy purpose. People who are called and chosen by God, by no merit of their own, are also consecrated. God does the choosing, God provides the grace to respond, and God consecrates. He consecrates through the Church He founded, and thus a religious sister professes vows to God which are received by the Church. These vows are public, not private, and this is important because a religious gives her life to God for the sake of others. She becomes a public figure, a representative of the Church. A vow is a deliberate and freely made promise made to God. In the case of a religious, the vows of poverty, chastity and obedience are her three-fold yes to God's invitation to follow Him more closely.

Visible and Stable Community Life

The second essential element in religious life is community. We are exhorted to be no less than "experts of communion."[72] This means that our relationships with one another are not an "extra-curricular," but a form of spirituality that religious are meant to cultivate and teach the world.[73] Religious communities should be characterized by true Christian charity; when they are, it is heaven on earth! The foretaste of this can be experienced in a myriad of simple ways. Sr. Ann Kateri experienced a taste of this very powerfully in the common human experience of moving. On two different occasions when she was reassigned from one convent to another, she had an opportunity to experience the bond of community. She reflected:

> Although both of these moves involved major shifts in responsibilities, they were so smooth, I distinctly remember marveling how incredibly loved I felt during them. I wasn't sure where the expression of genuine love was greater— from the sisters whom I was leaving or from the sisters who received me at the new convent. I wondered where else in the world is the experience of moving so encouraging and uplifting! Truly community has become family, and moving between convents simply living with different family members.

---

72   *Fraternal Life in Communion,* by the Congregation for Institutes of Consecrated Life and Societies of Apostolic Life, 10.

73   Pope John Paul II, *Vita Consecrata,* 46.

We learn from John's Gospel that the crowning point of human history will be when God draws us all together in Himself. As religious, we receive our communal life as a gift and a precursor of what is to come. Not that community life starts out as heaven on earth. It doesn't take a new postulant long to realize that all the sisters are still part of the fallen human race, with the rougher edges of their personality still being smoothed out. (And the new postulants will surely be part of the purification process!) In community, you can't just "grow apart" or "break up." You can't simply avoid the sister who irritates you. Community life is designed to turn sinners into saints, and that is done together. It is by staying in the game that the skills and techniques get perfected, and it is by committed relationships of self-giving love that the human person is sanctified.

Sr. Ana Chiara put it this way, "Before I entered, when I was out in the world, I just avoided people who made me angry. But here in the convent I couldn't do that, not if I wanted to live my vocation authentically. So I forgave, and I was forgiven, and I grew in real friendship. Community life is more than natural affection; it is a miracle." It is a miracle that the world desperately needs.

Evangelical Mission

The third essential element is evangelical mission, or the corporate apostolate. Religious women are engaged in a tremendously wide array of ministries and apostolates. Often teaching and nursing come to mind when you think of what sisters traditionally do. St. Teresa of Calcutta also made service of the poorest of the poor more widely known.

Certainly, sisters have always served as missionaries, proclaiming the Gospel in foreign lands, but there are many other missions open to women religious as well, such as evangelization through the media and care of the sick through medical ministry at the highest levels (including physicians of every discipline, from surgeons to psychiatrists). Sisters give retreats and run retreat houses; they serve the faithful through spiritual direction and campus ministry. Sisters minister to prisoners and prostitutes, and are working to end human trafficking. This list does not exhaust what sisters do, but it shows that within our common mission, the salvation of souls, there are many worthy ways to be a "laborer in the vineyard." Religious share in the mission of Jesus Himself. Whatever the apostolate of the community may be, it is at heart a sharing in the Father's will to save the world. The Father sends the Son for this purpose, and He calls each consecrated person to a special union with His Son and a sharing in His mission. It is important that the apostolate of an institute be true to its original charism. Religious seem to do best when they do what they were founded to do.

Prayer (Communal, Liturgical, and Personal)

A religious sister's prayer life did not begin when she entered the convent; she is in the convent *because* a rich prayer life led her there. As a religious, she no longer has to struggle to carve out times for prayer as she did before. Now prayer is built right into the schedule. The bell rings and the sisters gather to pray.

The prayer of a religious is of critical importance—it is our lifeline to God and the source of grace for everything else we do. Jesus Himself gave the example of relying on prolonged times of prayer for the sake of adoration of the Father, a prayer which Jesus invites us into.

Prayer has many dimensions in religious life. Liturgical prayer (Holy Mass and the Liturgy of the Hours) keeps the sister in the heart of the Church, praying with and for all the faithful. Religious communities pray at least some of the Liturgy of the Hours (or the Divine Office) in common as part of the daily rhythm of prayer. If you are not familiar with the Liturgy of the Hours, this is a prayer you will want to get to know in your discernment process. It is a way to sanctify the day by stopping and returning very deliberately and consciously to prayer with the whole Church, specifically by using the psalms. It is striking to realize that Jesus Himself prayed the psalms. When we pray the psalms even now, we join our prayers to His as we worship the Father.

But prayer must also be personal, and a religious sister needs time for personal prayer as well as for communal prayer. God is the source of our vocation and He calls us, first of all, to be with Him. Prayer is our means of *being* with Him.

The love I wish to express to Him in prayer is made real through my relationships within community. The kindness, compassion, and loving service shown to my sisters is an act of worship to God. And finally, the communion among the sisters overflows into the mission we were founded to accomplish. The variety of works done by religious sisters is staggering, and each is a reflection of a dimension of the life and mission of Jesus Christ. Prayer and work, done in community, are the rhythmic breath of the religious life.

As you visit communities, you will be joining in their

prayers, and you will experience firsthand the priority and importance that the community places on prayer. Many communities gather as many as five times a day to pray, and even more often in contemplative communities. In many communities, there is time built in for meditation, Eucharistic adoration, spiritual reading, and the rosary.

Asceticism

Asceticism, the fifth essential element, has to do with *externals*, such as what a religious has in her possession, what she eats and drinks, how often she fasts, and what she drives (or whether she drives), as well as how she uses technology and entertainment. A life of asceticism also entails an *internal* dimension which includes a simplicity and poverty of spirit, making the religious docile, humble, and other-oriented. A religious life with no austerity is almost a mockery, because as Christians we follow a God-Man who freely chose a life of simplicity, poverty, and ultimately suffering and death. Jesus told us clearly that to be His followers, we would be expected to pick up our own crosses and carry them daily. Religious have an even deeper obligation to live a life conformed to Christ than do others who are likewise called to holiness according to their state of life.

Have you ever wondered what the home of the Holy Family looked like? What kind of furnishings it had? What the dishes, linens, and wall hangings were like? With Joseph and Jesus being carpenters by trade, it's easy to imagine simple, well-made, beautiful furnishings in their home. Mary certainly had an eye for beauty, and even if their belongings were few, which is likely, it is easy to imagine everything was perfectly clean and artfully made. Simplicity and poverty are not in contradiction to dignity and beauty. Austerity and self-denial create a greater place within us for God to dwell.

Public Witness

"Of its nature, religious life is a witness that should clearly manifest the primacy of the love of God and do so with the strength coming from the Holy Spirit." So begins the passage on public witness in *Essential Elements*.[74]

Everything we do, the way we live, and what we wear should be a consistent proclamation of the Gospel. As Mother Mary Francis put it, "God is enough, and everything else is not enough." The life of a religious is meant to be infused with the Gospel values, the beatitudes. As you visit communities, you will notice how the sisters live and how they act. You are looking to join a group of women who are striving to be poor, simple, unworldly, kind, meek, and humble as Christ Himself was. It should show.

A religious is a public person and is meant to be entirely available to others. The Venerable Fulton J. Sheen's book on the priesthood is titled *The Priest is Not His Own*, and the same can be said of religious. This is why many religious choose to always wear the habit. It is a sign to you that we are available.

Relation to the Church

Wherever you go in search of a religious family, you are looking to make your home in the heart of the Church.

---

74   *Essential Elements*, 32.

Religious women are very much the heart of Holy Mother Church, manifesting in their lives the inner reality of what the Church is: Virgin, Bride, and Mother.

As you look at various communities, ask yourself, what is the community's disposition toward the Holy Father, toward the local bishop? How is religious obedience lived out in the community? Is there a clear superior? What is the relationship between the superior and the other sisters? Do you sense love, respect, and esteem? Does the superior seem to lead with a servant-leadership ideal? These are ideals put forth by the Church, and they are marks of a healthy Catholic religious community.

Formation

Formation is the training process that a woman goes through as she becomes a fully professed religious sister. Formation is meant to continue on throughout her life. It is easy to reduce our understanding of formation to academics alone. But in truth, formation touches upon every aspect of the person and uses a great variety of means to accomplish its end. When I was serving as our community's candidate and postulant directress, I would often tell the new class of candidates that they themselves were half of the formation of their classmates. The aspect of learning to live together, to get along with people who come from different backgrounds and life experiences, who see things differently and do things differently, requires plenty of virtue!

The schedule itself provides another major means of formation: getting up promptly, being at prayers (physically and mentally), and being present and ready for each portion of the day. This is how discipline grows and self-denial is achieved. The Sacraments are also an indispensable means of formation. Regular Confession and daily Mass provide the sacramental grace to change us substantially. The formator[75] chosen by God is the chief instrument of the Holy Spirit in the formation of a young sister. Regular conversations, characterized by openness and honesty, aid the young sister through encouragement, instruction, and the personalized accompaniment that is irreplaceable in the formation process.

As you visit, make inquiries into the formation process. What are the stages from entrance to final vows? These certainly will include a novitiate of at least one year and a period of temporary vows which will be between three and nine years (at most).

Government

Finally, the ninth essential component of religious life to note is the government of the institute. (Some aspects of government were discussed under Relation to the Church.) Faith is the guiding principle of our relationship to government. We exercise faith that God-given authority is also God-guided. And our faith assures us that our mature, freely given obedience is an act of worship to God. How is the community structured? How do permissions work? How

---

75   Whether it's the postulant director, the novice director, or the director of the sisters in temporary vows, the sister who has been assigned in the role of formation is responsible for the holistic training of the sisters in her care.

are superiors elected? These are all questions related to government.

It is not advisable to go into your first "come and see" visit like an investigative reporter, asking questions about elections and chapters. However, as your relationship with a particular community deepens, you will certainly want to ask to read the community's rule of life and constitutions, which are the primary inspirational and governing documents of a community. In so doing, you will get an idea of the governmental structure.

A religious detached from the guiding authority of the Church is like a "freelance" mercenary tossed about in search of the next cause in need of an activist. The life of a Catholic religious sister is necessarily yoked to the Church. It is born of the Church and guided by her authority. In turn, the religious is at the heart of the Church, showing forth tangibly her inner nature.

All religious communities share the same essential elements, but each community expresses and lives them uniquely—just as different artists using the same palette will each create a different masterpiece. The Church sets out guidelines, but God works differently through various founders and foundresses to inspire communities with remarkably diverse charisms.[76]

---

76   Every founder or foundress of a religious community was given a particular gift which is meant for building up the Church. This gift is the charism which is lived by the founder and passed down as a spiritual patrimony to the members who come later. The charism encompasses the special work that the community does, but it also touches upon every aspect of the community's life.

The fullness of the charism of any institute is difficult to adequately express in a few words. A charism is often reduced to a "mission statement" or web-page banner out of necessity, but it is always so much more. For example, a Franciscan Sister of the Renewal might say that her charism is "hands-on work with the poor and evangelization," and it is. But it is also characterized by a radical dependence on Divine Providence, by faithful devotion to the Holy Roman Catholic Church, and reverence for the Holy Father. It includes very special devotion to Jesus in the Eucharist and filial love of Our Blessed Mother Mary. And it would incomplete if we left out living Gospel simplicity with a warm family spirit. It is also characterized by deep relationships within a close-knit community, and an earthy simplicity that is just plain hard to put into words! And all of that is shot through with the Franciscan joy that lives on from one generation of Franciscans to the next. These features are felt and experienced better than explained.

Once a diocesan vocation director approached me with the idea of creating a "charism assessment" to help discerning women figure out to which community they were called—a kind of test to determine which family you belong in. Somehow I don't think it would work. Like Jesus said, "Come and see."

Chapter Ten

A Day in the Life

"Yours is the day and yours is the night"
~Psalm 74:16

Sweeping the sidewalk and picking up litter in front of the convent was one of my jobs when I first entered. I would try to time it so that I was out on the street around three o'clock when the school around the corner let out. The kids used to like to stop and sit on the steps and talk for a while on their way home. If I wasn't outside with the broom, they would often ring the bell on their way home to see if a sister could come out. I remember answering the door and coming out to see the kids standing there craning their necks to see what they could in the few moments the door to the convent was open. Sometimes we would hear them climb the steps and crouch down and try to peek through the mail slot! (What they saw was an eyeful of floor tiles and my sandaled feet as I opened the door.) They were filled with wonder, and they were filled with questions. This might also describe the way you feel, especially if you haven't yet made a "come and see" retreat to a convent.

Whether in the city or the country, whether teaching, caring for the poor, or living in a cloister, the pillars of life in any convent are the same: prayer, community, apostolate.

In the pages ahead you will get a detailed description of what goes on day-to-day in the religious life.

Our Lady Queen of Angels Convent, East Harlem, New York

> **Rising—5:15 a.m.** I rise and straighten the bedding on my wooden pallet, wash my face at the sink, and slip out into the darkened hallway. No other lights are on as I move quietly down the stairs, two floors to the chapel where the red glow from the sanctuary candle provides the only light. The Hidden Presence waits for my visit, and I linger there a moment as I offer my morning greeting in the utter stillness of this sanctuary on 113th Street, East Harlem, New York.

> **First Prayers—6:00 a.m.** Two sharp rings of the bell resonate throughout the convent. The lights in the chapel come on, the candles are lit, and one by one the sisters stream in. Being such creatures of habit, we usually arrive in the same order, day after day. Silent genuflections, a kiss for the floor, and in a moment's time, both choirs are full. The prayer leader knocks twice and Office of Readings begins. The first hour,

Office of Readings, consists of the recitation of the psalms and then two lengthy readings, the first from the Scriptures and the second from the early fathers of the Church, or a canonized saint whom we may be celebrating on a particular day. Kneeling on the wooden floor after Office, we pray the Memorare for the special intention that our community always be united in charity. Then, three Hail Marys for the sisters in the missions. As we pray, I let their faces emerge before my mind's eye: Sr. Jacinta, Sr. Monica, Sr. Veronica, Sr. Colette, Sr. Catherine, Sr. Elizabeth, Sr. Faustina, Sr. Chiara, and Sr. Josephine. This daily practice, simple as it is, keeps them close.

Meditation—6:20 a.m. The silence in the convent is sustained for the next hour, as we take our morning meditation time. (Outside the convent is another matter. The big truck that delivers milk for the school will pull in soon and make noisy work of the unloading. A car alarm sounds with tones so familiar that the local mockingbird does a perfect imitation! There is no street construction noise yet, and that is a small mercy. Learning to tune out the sounds of traffic on 2nd Avenue comes quickly. I am convinced that the human person can get used to *anything*.) Some sisters stay in the chapel; some return to their cell for this morning meditation hour.

Morning Prayer—7:30 a.m. Two rings of the bell summon all to the chapel again, now for Morning Prayer, the next installment of the Liturgy of the Hours. The prayer we offer together is the same prayer that rises up like incense from convents, monasteries, friaries, rectories, and presbyteries around the world; from novitiates and seminaries, bishops' residences and papal apartments, from homes and dorm rooms—even from subways, buses, and taxis, as many more of the laity have not only discovered the Divine Office but created new means to pray it more easily using smart phones and the like. United in this way with the whole Body of Christ, we offer Him ourselves as we sanctify the morning hours through this ancient prayer.

Holy Mass—8:00 a.m. Morning Prayer flows right into the Holy Sacrifice of the Mass. One of our friars has arrived during the meditation hour, and now he is vested and ready to make the Living God present for us anew. On this particular day, it is Father Andrew who emerges from the sacristy. Though a priest fifty years, this Mass, in our little chapel, for a congregation of nine sisters, is offered with the same thoughtful reverence of a first Mass of a newly ordained priest. These moments, so ordinary as part of our daily rhythm of life, provide the nucleus of our existence, the wellspring from which we live. Mass is finished and all linger; a prolonged thanksgiving crowns the morning.

chicken, and salad. Living by Divine Providence is truly an adventure because we relinquish control and trust in Him. But living by Divine Providence is not to be equated with meager fare or scraping to get by. God provides plenty to meet all our needs and plenty more for the needs of the poor we serve. Our poverty provokes the providence of God. Another way to say it is that our poverty lets God *father* us as He has desired to do from the beginning. After the blessing, the Gospel designated for the next day's liturgy is read. Dinner conversation is lively, with plenty to report from the day's activities.

Clean-up—7:15 p.m. Without a dishwasher (by design, of course) we wash, dry, and put away dishes three times a day. This makes us all expert dishwashers! Believe it or not, we consider doing the dishes an extension of our recreation. We continue all the lively antics of dinner, and plenty of laughter accompanies this typically mundane household chore. After dishes, there is still a little time in the day to complete some unfinished tasks or engage in an evening apostolate, such as a parish talk or a young adult event.

Rosary and Night Prayer—8:40 p.m. The voice of God resounds to us through the beloved bell, once again. We gather now for the fifth scheduled time of prayer. The lights are dim and we pray the holy rosary together with the melodious rhythm of people long accustomed to praying together as one voice, more or less. Then we pray Night Prayer, spiritually united with the world-wide Church, followed by the St. Michael Prayer and one more Marian hymn before silence falls on the convent again. Some sisters linger and pray, while others make a direct line for their cell. Morning comes quickly in the convent after all. Usually all lights are out by 10:30 p.m.

Epiphany House, Lincoln, Nebraska

Some fifteen hundred miles west of New York City in a convent of the Great Plains state of Nebraska, the new day begins in much the same way as in New York. While the routines and work are different in some ways, the staples of the life are the same for both. My friend, Sr. Mary Alma, who has been assigned to serve at a diocesan grade school and who lives at Epiphany House, the community's discernment house for young women, provided me with a detailed description of a day in the life of a School Sister of Christ the King in rural Nebraska.

Rising—5:15 a.m. Before the sun rises a School Sister of Christ the King is awakened by the sound of bell and a knock at the door which prompts her first words of the day, "Thanks be to God and Mary." A special prayer is said as the sister puts on each piece of her religious habit. Perhaps the most beautiful is the prayer for the ring which a professed sister wears on her left hand. "My King and my Spouse, let this ring ever remind me of my promise of perpetual fidelity and of Your spousal love for me." Jesus' spousal love is her rock foundation as she enters the new day.

Meditation—5:45 a.m. After putting her room in order, she makes her way to the chapel for quiet meditation. This is a precious time where heart speaks to Heart. It is not car alarms which compete for the sisters' attention, but rather the peaceful sound of the mourning dove and an occasional hoot of the great horned owl that lives in the oak tree east of the convent.

Morning Prayer—6:15 a.m. After Lauds,[80] the same morning prayer that is prayed in New York City and in hundreds of convents dotting the U.S. map,[81] the sister has breakfast with her community, cleans up, gathers her school bags, and makes one last visit to Jesus in the Blessed Sacrament before piling in the car with her fellow sisters to head for school, which in this case is exactly one rosary away.

Arrival at School—7:30 a.m. Upon arriving

---

80   Originally the Hours were referred to exclusively by their Latin names. You might hear sisters going back and forth between the Latin and English.

81   See the Demographics section at www.cmswr.org to see an actual U. S. map so dotted.

and before entering the classroom or office, the first stop is always the church to once again tell Jesus of her love and more importantly to receive His. The sister will almost always mention some child, such as Vincent, who is in special need. She begs the Lord for the grace to be open and attentive to the promptings of the Holy Spirit; she invites her Mother Mary to continue to teach her how to be a warm and tender spiritual mother while working with the children throughout the day. According to Sr. Mary Alma, beginning the school day is a whirlwind of love in action as she gathers her children and brings them to the classroom. They will be together for the next seven hours and thirty minutes. Lunch count must be taken, homework collected, notes from home read, and items brought to the office. At the same time, the sister is noticing each child. Juli looks good and is smiling. Carter forgot his lunch. Perla is not here yet, but she is often late. Luz looks a little pale and is unusually quiet this morning. "I'll have her sit by me at Mass," sister decides. She hears a crash in the coat area. It is Vincent underneath a stack of books. It is easy to see how the gift of spiritual maternity has the opportunity to come to the fore each day for a teaching sister!

Holy Mass—8:15 a.m. Next is Holy Mass, which the children attend each day before the academic portion of their schooling. There is something truly beautiful about participating in Holy Mass with the little ones, says Sr. Mary Alma: "There is something of a foretaste of heaven about it. The Kingdom of God, after all, belongs to little children."

Teaching Apostolate—9:00 a.m. By now the reading, writing, and arithmetic have begun. The sister is responsible for teaching these children with their full array of needs. She is intensely aware that three have special education needs, two are about two grades below grade level, and two others are gifted intellectually, reading four or five grades above their age level. One of the bright ones is on the autism spectrum and needs to walk in a figure-eight pattern in the back of the room to calm down from time to time. There are other challenges too: "Janice tends to tattle and Brian routinely gets caught in bouts of self-pity. Vincent can't seem to make it through a recess without losing his temper and declaring the world grossly unfair. He lives with his uncle. Neither he nor we at school know much about his actual parents. Jose's father had to return to Mexico last year. The family does not know when they will see him again." Sister holds all these things in her heart as she presents her lesson on possessive pronouns and tries to patiently correct Vincent for throwing an eraser across the room. How can anyone manage all this? There is always another Teacher in the room with her and Sister puts her trust in Him. Though continually challenging, it is at the same time a joy and a privilege to spend herself for the formation of young souls in the likeness of Christ.

School Day Ends—3:20 p.m. Sister traces the Sign of the Cross in blessing on the foreheads of her students as they say goodbye and get into their cars or bus lines. What's this? Vincent forgot his homework again! Faculty meetings, parent phone calls, paper correcting, and final adjustments to the next day's lesson plans are the next order of the day. The time goes quickly, but not so fast as to prevent another visit to Jesus in the Blessed Sacrament or perhaps to pray the Stations of the Cross, a daily part of a CK sister's life. The car ride home provides a moment to relax from the flurry of the day and a gradual transition from that activity of the apostolate to a time of prayer spent with her Spouse at the evening Holy Hour.

Holy Hour—5:30 p.m. Once again, this is precious time in which sister's heart goes to her Beloved. The Blessed Sacrament is exposed for adoration, and sister gratefully enters into the silence and union with her King. The Holy Hour closes with the communal worship of God at Vespers and reposition of the Blessed Sacrament.

Dinner—6:30 p.m. Sister enjoys an evening

meal with her community. Whether the convent is in New York or Nebraska, there is laughter around the table! Dinner conversation is light-hearted, with funny escapades of the children being recounted. At times the conversation flows naturally to spiritual topics, with sister sharing something from her spiritual reading or how the Lord has touched her heart during the day. Sometimes she will share a struggle or a burden with her sisters in Christ. They listen well and offer their loving support. Evening meals are a priceless time of community.

Personal Time—7:40 p.m. Dinner is over by this time, and all the dishes are washed and put away. Laundry is folded, and lunches are made for the next day. With the remaining two hours, depending on the evening, the sister may have some extra free time for a walk or some other exercise, time to work together on a needed community project, clean the convent, help a sister with something she needs to have completed for the next day, play a game, or have more time for personal prayer or rest. As the evening lengthens, sister completes the final tasks of the day, such as ironing her habit or taking one last look in preparation for tomorrow's lessons and activities. She will prepare the Scripture readings for the next day's Mass, pray Compline, and talk over her day with the Lord in her Examen prayer.

Grand Silence—10:00 p.m. A holy silence pre-
vails in the convent as sister retires with prayer
in her heart. Sleep comes easily. What a joy it is
to belong totally to Christ the King and spend
yourself completely that He may reign in all
hearts!

Having walked through a day in the life of two communities, perhaps you found your imagination pondering the
sisters whose lives these pages represent. Does everybody
in the convent keep this schedule? What does it feel like in
"week one" and what does it feel like after twenty years?

I can remember the torture it was to get up early every
day in the beginning. I would slide into Office of Readings
just in time. I was grateful that we prayed in choirs (alternat-
ing reading the psalm out loud from side to side) so I could
rest my eyes when the other side was reading. The life was
challenging in every way, and yet I was happier and more
at peace than I had ever been. Twenty years later I wake up
before my alarm and I am wide awake at Office of Readings,
but I remember it didn't start out that way.

Chapter Eleven

What a Community is Looking for in You

Y ou might be thinking, "If I am going to the trouble to renounce the whole world, any community ought to throw open the doors and receive me! What's there to think about?" It is the condition of youth to think about everything from their position. The thought that the community has its *own* discernment to make is like a twist in the plot. I'll admit this idea came as a complete surprise to me, too!

When you pause to think about it, though, it makes perfect sense. Sisters only want women to join who are genuinely called by God, women who will thrive in the convent, women who will become saints by living out the charism with them. Ultimately, it is for your good that the community does its discernment well.

So who would make a good sister? The danger in putting this down in print is that the reader might see the ideal, and finding herself wanting, dismiss the possibility as unattainable. This would be a mistake. As Christians, we look to the Gospels for a blueprint for discipleship. If we were to read the ideal and dismiss it as unattainable without even trying, where would we be two thousand years after the Resurrection? No, we do "our lousy best" (to borrow a phrase from Servant of God Fr. Walter Cizcek, S.J.) and let God make up what is lacking in us.

The other danger in trying to articulate what it takes to become a sister is that it could foster a notion that we can do something to merit or achieve a religious vocation. Not so. A call originates in God. Only He decides, for His own mysterious reasons, who is called. We cannot muster up a call by enough prayer or desire. However, by our own free will, we have an opportunity to choose to say yes to His fatherly plans.

With that in mind, we will take an honest look at what basic characteristics should be present, even if they are not fully developed, for a woman to pursue religious life in maturity and in freedom. Here are seven things that vocation directors are usually hoping to find in a candidate:

1. A call initiated by God

2. A personal relationship with God consisting of a regular prayer life and sacramental practice (probably for three or more years)

3. Genuine desire for the religious life and a free response to the call

4. Good health: physical, psychological, and emotional

5. Maturity required to live common life and to make a sincere gift of self

6. Desire and capacity for living out poverty, chaste celibacy, and obedience

7. An interest and desire for the specific charism of the institute

1) How Do I Know If This Is a Call from God?

Motivation is very important. What is moving you to discern religious life? If you are talking to a vocation director because your pious aunt had a dream and in the dream you were in a religious habit, or because your long-term boyfriend just broke up with you to apply to seminary, or because you promised St. Thérèse you would become a Carmelite if she helped you pass your final exams, or because you heard a homily in which the priest said that every young adult owed it to the Church to consider a vocation to priesthood or religious life and duty compels you—then slow down, because none of these motives provides convincing evidence of a call. Another motivation that can come into play is self-inflicted penance. This can happen when a woman commits a serious sin, has great difficulty forgiving herself, and then tries to make it up to God by taking on a self-imposed penance to do the hardest thing she can think of, like entering religious life. This motivation is usually unconscious, and the person is totally unaware of it until it is pointed out as a possibility.

How can you know if you have a call initiated by God? It will come from within and not from without. And if it does come from outside yourself, it will be as a confirmation of what already exists in your own heart (buried though the desire may be). The human heart can be compared to a beautiful rose. When the bud is tightly closed, you cannot speed along the process of blooming by peeling the petals back. Your "helping" destroys the rose. If your heart is not opening naturally to discerning a call, do not force it. A call is a very personal thing, between God and you. I don't think God wants you to be wrangled into discernment by guilt trips. If you begin to feel your heart opening to the possibility, follow a plan for discernment and pay special attention to your thoughts, feelings, and desires, especially in times of consolation, which is how you will begin to notice authentic indicators of a call.[82]

Sr. Ann Kateri's discernment process provides a beautiful example of God Himself opening the rose. She first felt the call at eleven or twelve years old, and she understandably decided that it was to be put off for a later date. Her Visitation high school years came and went, then her Harvard University years came and went. She moved back to the Washington, D.C. area and started working as a youth minister. She was serving the poor and living an active social life. Her original vocational call was fading in the background, and her heart was becoming more and more set on marriage. Her young adult life was full and fun, and finally she found herself engaged to be married as she had earnestly desired.

It was only upon becoming engaged that she realized that her original call from childhood was still there. "A deep sadness came over me, and I couldn't eat or sleep," she remembers. She went to a priest she knew well for counsel,

---

82   *Discerning the Will of God* (Crossroad Publishing) by Fr. Timothy Gallagher, OMV, will be an important book for you and your spiritual director in assessing the authenticity of your call.

and he advised her to take a six-month break from the relationship. She felt convicted that this was the most reasonable thing to do.

Reasonable? Yes. Easy? No. "Taking that ring off my finger and walking away from the relationship was the hardest thing that I've ever had to do," she said. She experienced sadness, yes, but also a deep peace. And as time went on, the sadness diminished and the peace grew. Sr. Ann Kateri had an experience of the Lord lovingly pursuing her, and the peace and joy in her own heart is the undeniable sign that she accepted the right proposal! She professed her final vows on June 28, 2014.

2) Personal Relationship with God

A religious vocation is a deepening of a relationship that already exists, beginning with your baptism.[83] The vocation director will be looking to see evidence of this developing relationship. I have encountered, more than once, what I'll call the "retreat-high discernment syndrome." This is when someone has a powerful experience on a retreat and immediately assumes she is being called to be a sister. She imagines, in her zeal, being fitted for her veil and signing her application on the dotted line. This would be like going out on one spectacular date and running away to elope. Every person is called to holiness, to deep intimacy with the Lord, and in fact, to become a saint. Sometimes, the first sweet taste of encounter, which is always an invitation to more, is

---

83   "Before they are admitted to the novitiate, candidates must show proof of baptism, confirmation, and free status." Canon 645.1.

mistaken for a call to consecrated life.

Another thing that happens is what I'll call the "intellectual discernment syndrome." This is when you learn more
about your faith and about religious life, maybe reading a
little bit of St. Thomas Aquinas, and loving everything that
you're discovering, leap to the conclusion that you certainly must be called to religious life. This is discernment in the
head, not in the heart. The head and heart must be in league
for good discernment.

True and trustworthy discernment flows from relationship; you can't have a relationship with an idea or a book.
You can only have a relationship with a person. If it's God's
will you want to discover, it is God you must be in relationship with. Developing your relationship with God through
prayer is essential. The boy is not going to ask you to marry
him if you haven't gone out on a date with him yet! How are
you going to know if God is calling you if you aren't listening
to Him in prayer?

A consistent prayer life is an important aspect of your
discernment process. However, understand that a vocation
director is not looking for a perfect prayer life. She is looking to see that even if you struggle to do it, you are trying to
make prayer a priority in your life.

A vocation director is also going to be looking for a few
years of sacramental intensity. Living the religious life requires preparation, which is perhaps best demonstrated by
living out your faith well in the world before attempting to
do it in the rarefied context of the convent. It's like running a
marathon. Despite the advice of the Nike commercials, most
people can't decide to "just do it," and expect to run the next

NYC marathon. You must walk before you run.

3) Desire for the Religious Life

Whenever I ask a young woman what she wants, what her true desires are, very often the answer comes, "I just want to do God's will." Let's set that aside for now. Doing the will of God is the overarching desire that moves you as a Christian, and that is as it should be. But take some time to look within. What do *you* want? If, in the process of discernment you never get to a point where you can say as St. Francis did, "This is what I desire; this is what I long for with all my heart!" then why are you going forward? God, our Father, created His children in freedom, with freedom, for freedom. Your life's vocation is meant to be chosen by you in freedom. You must want it and choose it.

In the beginning, at the first thought of a religious vocation, you may not be able to say that you sincerely desire it. This is not surprising. The important thing is that somewhere along the path of prayer and discernment, which includes visiting religious communities and growing in relationship with sisters, the desire grows within you to the point at which you can sincerely say that you *want* this vocation—that it is the desire of your heart.

Again, we can look to human relationships for an analogy. If the young man you're dating proposes marriage by saying, "I've been praying about it and I know that God wants us to be married. Will you be my wife?" I don't know any sane woman who would say yes to that. He thinks he knows what God wants, but what does *he* want? That is not the proposal you've been dreaming of because that's not the proposal you were made for. You want to hear him say, "I love you. I can't imagine my life without you. You are my reason for my being on this earth. I want to love and cherish you forever. Will you marry me?" Now *that* is a proposal you could say yes to! But imagine that you responded to such a heartfelt proposal with, "Since I have prayed about it, and I am nearly certain that this is God's will for my life, I will say yes." We are made to make a free gift of self to another. In the act of self-giving, we realize the happiness and the true joy we were made for. God wants no less. If He "proposes" to you, He wants to hear you say a yes that comes from your heart, from the core of your being, from the depths of your freedom.

This emphasis on desire can be confusing. It seems that we are meant to follow some desires and not others. We desire one thing and then are called to something else. Yet we are told God places the desires in our heart, and He means to fulfill them.[84] How to make sense of this question? In my own experience, I can say that at one point in my life I desired marriage and children, and I did not desire religious life. At this point in my life, obviously, I can say I desire religious life, and I do not desire marriage anymore; I'm already given to another. If our vocation is planted like a seed in our hearts, why don't we want it from the beginning?

The seed is there, buried in the soil of the heart, and there are a lot of layers to break through for that seed to sprout. The natural desires for marriage and children are

---

84   St. Thérèse of Lisieux, in her letter to her sister Marie dated September 17, 1896, writes, "God never gives desires that He cannot realize." *Story of a Soul* (Saint Benedict Press), 163. However, the way in which these desires are realized can be different than first expected.

usually right on the surface, not at all hard to get in touch with. It's only in going deeper that I can get at the truest, most real desire of my inmost heart. What if the seed is not getting water and sunlight, prayer, and true teaching? What if there are toxins in the soil and not nutrients?

I think Jesus's parable about the seed can be applied to the question of vocation. Jesus Himself says the seed is the Word, and we can see it as the Word of our own identity sown into our hearts. "A sower went out to sow his seed. And as he sowed, some seed fell on the path and was trampled, and the birds of the sky ate it up." I wonder how often a religious vocation has been trampled because instead of the rich soil of the heart being protected and safeguarded, it was used and abused.

"Some seed fell on rocky ground, and when it grew, it withered for lack of moisture." I wonder how many religious vocations have been unable to grow because of false teachings, bad example, or no example.

"Some seed fell among thorns, and the thorns grew and choked it." How many religious vocations got choked out by the toxic climate of American youth culture, by entertainment, materialism, pornography, and crisis of identity, just to name a few of the toxins?

"And some seed fell on good soil, and when it grew, it produced fruit a hundredfold." We hear about the hundredfold in another place, when Peter wanted to know what exactly the reward was going to consist of for himself and the other apostles who had given up everything to follow Him. Jesus assured Peter that "Everyone who has given up houses or brothers or sisters or father or mother or children or lands for the sake of [His] name will receive a hundred times more, and will inherit eternal life" (Luke 8:4-15).

It seems that there are many things that can prevent our vocation from growing within us, but when it does grow and you freely choose the identity God chose for you, watch out! The blessings will be abundant.

4) Good Health[85]

Along with a call from God and a desire on your part, the physical capacity to live religious life is also required. This principle is true for other life choices as well. If you're afraid of flying, don't sign up for pilot school. If the sight of blood makes you faint, a medical profession may not be the best fit for you. Both active and contemplative religious life entails a somewhat rigorous schedule. It includes getting up early virtually every day, and at least some fasting and austerities of different kinds. (In our community, based in the Bronx, some of the austerities have to do with sirens and music at all hours, as well as traffic and pollution.)

In every community, the circumstances of the life itself will have different built-in penances which will serve as a test of capacity. Religious sisters live in community, share things in common, and have little choice in many matters. Being a religious makes you a public person, living vows of poverty, chastity, and obedience in the context of a religious community with whom you live and work. This requires self-discipline and simplicity of life. In other words, if you

---

85   Canon 642 requires that superiors admit only those who have the required health, suitable character, and sufficient maturity.

are too "high maintenance," it may not work out for you.

It is necessary not only to be healthy (by all measures: physically, psychologically, and emotionally), but also to be well-integrated and mature. Plus, it also helps if you have a sense of humor. The application process will bear these things out, but you should know the expectations from the start. Some health problems which would be considered prohibitive in many communities would be emotional illnesses such as bipolar disorder, chronic depression, and anxiety disorders. Chronic conditions or diseases which require expensive or time-consuming treatments would also be prohibitive in many communities. Even less severe conditions (including dietary restrictions), which would require you to be exempted from some facet of the common life would be, at the very least, a point of further evaluation with the community.

5) Maturity

Firstly, according to canon law, a woman must have reached her seventeenth year prior to entering the novitiate.[86] Canon law does not specify an upper age limit. However, many communities have age thirty or thirty-five as an upper age limit. This is because it is more difficult to submit to formation at older ages. However there are a few religious

---

86   Code of Canon Law, 643

communities that accept older vocations.[87]

Human maturity is not something that is arrived at like a twenty-first birthday or a graduation day. Maturation is a life-long process, and we are never meant to be through with it. To either enter religious life or to marry, a certain level of maturity should be reached. How do you know if you are mature enough to make a life choice? Here are some indicators of readiness. You should be able to:

- Look at your past and take personal responsibility for your actions, while also forgiving wrongs done to you.

- Be self-motivated: have the ability to make plans or decisions and carry them out.

- Maintain a grateful disposition and not take people or other blessings for granted.

- See beyond your own needs to the needs of others, initiating help before being asked.

- Be self-reflective, share of yourself vulnerably, and make a sincere gift of self.

- Give and receive mercy by apologizing sincerely and accepting the sincere apology of another.

These items can serve for a self-exam. If you're unsure about your own development in any area, ask a close friend or family member who will be honest with you, especially someone you live with. It should be noted that these are

---

87   Among communities that may receive older vocations are: All Saints Sisters of the Poor, Servants of the Lord and the Virgin Matara, Eudist Servants of the Eleventh Hour, Daughters of Divine Hope, Visitation Nuns of Mobile, Alabama

qualities to be growing in; you should not expect to have all of them fully developed yet!

Religious life is intensely communal.[88] Each sister is called to fully give herself in relationship and in service for the other and for the mission. You don't choose your sisters like you chose your friends at school. Community life is made up of every known Myers-Briggs combination, all the temperaments included. To be mature enough to enter means to be ready to put up with yourself and to put up with others for the long-haul of sanctification, to deny yourself, take up your cross daily, and follow Jesus.

6) Desire and Capacity for the Vows

When discerning religious life, the renunciation required can be breathtaking. To even consider chastity, for example, could make you feel that the breath was knocked clean out of you! I remember feeling that way. Giving up having your own family is a massive consideration and can pose a major obstacle in moving forward toward a call to religious life. In the discernment process, it is difficult to even

---

88   Those who struggle with same-sex attraction may wonder if religious life is an option. This question must be discerned on an individual basis with a spiritual director, but some general statements can be made. If a woman has a homosexual orientation which is consistent and deeply rooted, religious life would not be recommended because it entails an intense fraternal living situation with people of the same sex. A living environment where some members are subjected to a disproportionate level of temptation would be unnecessarily difficult for the person. It probably would be advisable to discern other forms of consecration which do not require communal living.

consider the benefits of chastity, the gift of a celibate life. At first we are so focused on whom we are *not* marrying that we can't yet see our way clear to notice or fully appreciate Whom we *are* marrying! The positive gift of chastity is necessarily obscured at first because the sacrifice required is so great that nothing else can be seen. That's the way it is at first. But by the time you have grappled with these things and walked far enough down the road of discernment to be applying for entrance, you should be able to see the sacrifice *and* the gift. You should be past focusing only on the gift that you are making and be able to consider the gift that God is making to you. Not that you are expected to fully understand it, but you should at least be able to see it.

Beginning to see yourself in a new bond with Christ is important. Perhaps this is a new idea for you, and you may wonder how it is that a religious could be considered a bride of Christ. The Old Testament is replete with bridal imagery. God is the Bridegroom and His people are His bride. In the New Testament, the nuptial imagery continues, only now the Incarnate Word is the Bridegroom and the Church is the bride. Since the first days of the Church, starting with St. Paul, the individual virgin has also been seen as the bride and Christ as the Bridegroom. Also, the contemplative person who reaches transforming union is also said to be in a "mystical marriage" with Christ. Interestingly, only the consecrated virgin can be bride in all four senses. That is, she is part of the people of God in the Old Testament sense. She is part of the Church in the New Testament sense. She is an individual virgin espoused to God in the Pauline sense. And finally, she aspires to contemplative union or the mystical marriage in the fourth sense, in which the bridal terminology is typically used. Yes, the religious sister can accurately be called the bride of Christ, as the Church has affirmed in her liturgical tradition and in her teaching for centuries.

In his 1995 letter to women, St. John Paul II highlights the value the spousal dimension of our call has for the whole Church. "Thank you, consecrated women! Following the example of the greatest woman, the Mother of Jesus Christ, the Incarnate Word, you open yourselves with obedience and fidelity to the gift of God's love. You help the Church and all mankind to experience a "spousal" relationship to God, one which magnificently expresses the fellowship which God wishes to establish with his creatures."[89]

As you discern, do not neglect the intellectual aspect of the process. To make a free choice, you must know what you are choosing. At the end of this book there is a short reading list to help you continue in your preparation.

7) Interest and Desire for the Specific Charism of the Institute

When God created you, He made you for something very specific. The community God has chosen for you will be right for you in who the sisters are *and* in what they do. While the work is less important than the call to belong to God,[90] the work is still important; in fact, it's rather artificial

---

89   Pope John Paul II, *The Genius of Woman* (USCCB).

90   "Jesus went up the mountain and summoned those whom He wanted and they came to Him" (Mark 3:13). Clearly, Jesus places the priority on the relationship over the work in the Apostolic life.

to separate the two. What you are is expressed in what you do. The mission will be the means by which you pour your love and self-sacrifice out for the salvation of the world with, in, and through Christ. If the mission is teaching, then the classroom will be the altar of your daily sacrifice. If nursing, then the hospital room will be your altar.

It is important for you to realize that the apostolate of an institute can be learned. You need not have previous experience or training, and if at the beginning you don't even have a strong interest and desire, it does not necessarily mean you are not called there. One sister in our community, now in final vows, was intensely attracted to the evangelization aspect of our apostolate, but the hands-on work with the poor held no appeal for her. Everything about her lengthy discernment process pointed toward entering. Her call was confirmed by her spiritual director and by the community, and yet she knew there was one piece missing. Not long into her formation she had an experience serving a homeless person who came to our door. She had a profound experience of Christ so vividly that she knew the missing piece had been found. Everything isn't harvested from the garden at once. Some fruits come early, and some come later. It's a process.

When applying to a community, there are three possible answers you could hear: "Yes!" "No," or "Not yet".

If you get a "No," accept it as the will of God, as God setting you free for another purpose. It is important to remember the foundational principle we established at the beginning: God is a loving Father, and He has a wonderful plan for you that will bring about your joy, His glory, and the salvation of souls. If God's will is for you to be in a certain community, you will *both* know it. Choose now to trust that God is working through the sisters with whom you are discerning.

If you get a "Not yet," listen attentively to the guidance the vocation director is giving you. She has a reason for delaying your entrance, and it is certainly with your growth and development in mind. Sometimes a person needs more time to heal or more time to develop their prayer life or perhaps their communication and interpersonal skills. Trust me, whatever the need for further development, it will be far easier to give yourself the space to grow outside the convent than inside the convent. Coming too soon can lead to frustration and feelings of inadequacy and even leaving the convent.

If you receive a "Yes," then it's time to start telling family and friends and preparing yourself for entrance, the topic of the next chapter.

Chapter Twelve

Preparing for Entrance

I f your discernment journey leads you to apply for entrance and you hear "yes" coming from all directions—your own heart and the community—it's time to get going!

When Jesus saw Levi sitting at his desk, Jesus simply said "follow me" and Levi got up and followed Jesus. There are no details given about informing his landlord or packing an overnight bag. He got up and followed Jesus. Those two words, "follow me," can be a motto to remember if you start getting bogged down in the details as you move through the weeks or months leading up to your entrance date. It's all about getting up and following Jesus.

Spiritual Preparation

Naturally there will be some things that need attention as you plan to begin this next phase of life. Preparing yourself to enter a religious community begins as your discernment began, with prayer. Have you ever had friends who were preparing for their wedding day? Being consumed with the details and the planning, they seem to talk of nothing else! It can be like that for you and the Lord. Over these months (or years) of discernment, your prayer has likely been consumed by the big vocation question and little else. I remember traveling back to Franciscan University after I finally had become a sister, and praying in the adoration chapel where I had spent so many anguished hours wrestling with God about my future. Returning as a sister brought a torrent of memories, and yet praying there now was blissfully peaceful because my prayer was *agenda-free*! It is vitally important for you to have prayer times that are agenda-free. Let the Lord lead in prayer. Listen to Him. Go where He wants to go.

You may consider incorporating a portion of the Liturgy of the Hours—perhaps morning and evening prayer—so as to begin to grow in familiarity with this prayer which will become an increasingly large part of your regular prayer when you enter. Another way to prepare your heart is by immersing yourself in the Gospels. The Gospel is the ultimate rule of life for all religious. You want to be *filled* with the life-giving Word. One way to prepare is to read the Gospels with the disposition of a bride-to-be listening to family stories about her fiancé.

Another good practice to begin even now is choosing to say yes again every day. This is a way of being conscious of the choice you're making, and also of strengthening your resolve, especially in the face of different temptations which will certainly arise. I know one sister who was assailed with temptations over the two weeks directly before her entrance. Even an old boyfriend from across the country suddenly emailed her out of the clear blue. She shared that pausing in front of that email, with the possibility of that relationship before her, was an important moment to choose Christ again.

Family and Friends

Another aspect of preparation has to do with your relationships. When to start talking about your discernment with family and friends can be a delicate question. Everyone's situation is different. Most young women have a natural instinct to conceal and protect their vocation in the very beginning. If you think of your call like a tender little plant just beginning to emerge from the soil, it's easy to see that the plant is very vulnerable and in need of safeguarding. As you first begin to discern, you have more questions than answers, along with plenty of fears and hopes, so it seems prudent to guard the little plant of your vocation until it has grown stronger and you have more confidence.

Usually, once a young woman feels fairly certain that she is being called, she will naturally begin to want to share this with the people closest to her. It is a good idea to let your parents and other close family and friends share in your discernment journey. I know one sister who did not share anything with her parents along the way until the last minute, and once she entered religious life, she regretted not being more forthcoming with them. Remember, your family and friends have their own journey to make in coming to terms with your vocation. You can make it easier for them by sharing with them and by answering their questions. Once you get to the point of visiting communities you likely would have told the people closest to you. Once you've been accepted, you may consider making a short list of people you hope to tell personally, and plan to speak with them yourself before they hear your news elsewhere.

When you feel the time is right to reveal your intentions to your parents and closest family, try to proceed with great sensitivity to their feelings. Put yourself in their shoes and try to understand the difficulties they may undergo accepting your vocation. Be sure to reflect beforehand on the many things you are grateful for, and make it a point to thank your parents for giving you the gift of life, for passing on the faith to you, and so on. It's likely that one conversation will not be adequate; you'll want to let them know you will do your best to answer their questions as they come up. You may consider showing them the community's website so they can get a glimpse for themselves until they have the opportunity to meet the sisters in person. Convey to them that you understand their feelings (perhaps sadness, disappointment, a feeling of loss, or maybe even grief), but also communicate your joy and peace. Usually, when parents see their child truly happy, it is a great satisfaction to them.

By the way, some parents are exceedingly happy to discover that their child has a religious vocation! And many parents who do not start out happy end up elated. Allow your parents the freedom to make their peace with your decision at their own pace.

If your parents do not approve of your vocation, it is likely because they feel that they are losing you. It can be difficult for parents to let go of their children no matter what vocation their child is called to, but religious life is especially difficult because parents know they will see less of you in the convent. There could be a variety of experiences contributing to the disapproval you're receiving from your parents, especially if they are not practicing the faith, have unresolved problems with the Church, or have had a bad experience with a sister at some time in their life. Pray for your parents. God has a plan for their healing, sanctification, and peace. Ultimately, though, you are not responsible for your parents' reaction or feelings. Even if they oppose your decision, it is a higher good to follow God's will for your life than to succumb to pressures (however well-meaning) that would deter you from your true vocation.

It might seem a small consolation, but I do not know of any communities who do not allow for family visits. It's good to share this with your parents so they can look forward to it. The customs for this vary from community to community, but an annual visit home is common. Some communities allow for a trip home for very significant family events as well, such as a wedding, ordination, or serious sickness in the family. It is not uncommon for religious sisters to return home for a short time to help care for a parent who becomes critically ill. Every situation is unique and would be discerned with the superior.

Communities typically allow for a certain number of letters each month and some communities allow a certain number of phone calls home, usually to parents. It is typical for community newsletters and Christmas cards to be sent to friends and family. The periodic visits home are also opportunities to keep up with old friends.

There is no doubt about it, relationships change. The amount of contact diminishes, and yet you can be sure that a religious sister remains connected with loved ones in a spiritual way—especially in the Eucharist. The relationships change, but don't end, and your family will be blessed by your vocation.

Material Matters

The time before entrance allows for clearing away financial obstacles. If you have an outstanding student loan, for example, you will need to make a plan for paying off your debt, either by working, seeking outside assistance, or both. Each situation is different.

Because most communities require candidates to be debt-free when they enter, there are organizations that were founded to help young people raise funds so they can enter religious life.[91] If you are faced with this challenge, you certainly would do well to speak to your pastor about it. Chances are he will have ideas of ways to support you. I know of more than one young woman who raised the needed funds through speaking at the Masses in her parish and then taking up a collection. One young lady I know raffled off a cow to clear her debt.

Reaching out to various Catholic organizations known to support vocations is a worthwhile endeavor. There are so many people in the Church who have been praying for an increase in religious vocations for a long time. These good people often feel blessed and privileged to assist someone who is taking steps toward the convent. However, proceed

---

91   Two such organizations are Mater Ecclesiae and The Labouré Society.

with sensitivity in this area and be sure to discuss any financial matters with your spiritual director.

Addressing debt can be overwhelming, but every seeming obstacle is another opportunity to place your trust more fully in God. If He is calling you, He will make a way for you. Nothing is beyond Him. As Mother Teresa used to say, "God has plenty of money!"

In addition to being debt-free when you enter, there may be expenses to consider such as health insurance. Some communities ask women entering to cover their first year of health insurance premiums, with the successive years covered by the community. Also, whatever the community expects you to bring with you when you enter will need to be purchased. Consider these needs carefully as you prepare.

What *do* you bring with you when you enter the convent? Not much! The community will provide you with a list of what to bring once you have been accepted to enter. If you've seen the BBC film *Young Nuns*, you'll remember the scene of Clara and her mother shopping for the items on her convent list. The mother and daughter duo are in a department store tiptoeing down the aisle shopping for slippers that will be quiet enough for a cloister!

The items on that list will vary from community to community, but it will have the specific clothes you need, the books needed, and whatever else is required or permitted, such as a musical instrument or sporting equipment. Certain things you might be permitted to bring to the convent, but the item (such as a basketball or guitar) may be held in common to be used by the whole community.

This leads to the question of getting rid of things before

entering the convent. How much should go? When you enter a religious community to begin your formation, although you have made a profound step toward becoming a religious, you are not one yet. Religious life begins with the novitiate. And even as a novice, you will not yet be bound by the vows. It is not until perpetual profession that the religious fully renounces ownership of property, and she signs a last will and testament which is binding in civil law as well as in canon law.[92] It is not advisable to make a dramatic renunciation of all your assets when you first enter. You could, however, sell your car and other smaller possessions as an act of renouncing the world and making a commitment to the Lord whom you truly think is calling you to follow Him just as He did the rich young man. In all of these matters, the specific community you're entering will have norms in place to guide you.

Preparing for a Life of Service

It may take a few months or it may take a few years from the time of firm decision to crossing over the threshold of the convent. Even though it may feel like you already have much to do to prepare yourself, try not to get so focused on yourself, your preparation, your family, and your needs that you forget others. Remember, you are about to give your whole life to God and to His people. Having opportunities to serve during this interim is a wonderful way to stay grounded in your first love. Certainly soup kitchens and food pantries would be glad to have a volunteer, but even the simple

---

92   Canon 668, 1.

acts of loving service to family and neighbors is a fine way to train your heart toward others.

Protecting Your Vocation

Another thing to consider as you prepare to enter is protecting your vocation as a precious gift from God. Be careful of what you are doing with your time. Is the entertainment you seek, the clothing you wear, and the company you keep consistent with the life choice you are about to make? If you go out with friends, ask yourself afterwards if you could have taken the sisters with you. It's not that you have to attempt to live the religious life at home before you enter, but you want to be consistent within yourself as you prepare for the transition you are about to make.

Let Your Light Shine

This time before entrance is also time to give witness! Your closely guarded secret no longer must be kept. If you have applied to a religious community and been accepted, now is the time to share the good news! (Even beyond your closest family and friends.) You'll want to share with extended family and others. Your pastor and perhaps your university chaplain would be happy to know of your choice. You also should consider letting your Diocesan Vocation Director know as well as the Diocesan Delegate for Religious (or Vicar for Religious).

The Church wants to rejoice with you in your vocation. Letting others know serves other purposes as well. Other young women in your parish and diocese will be inspired by your "yes" and may consider a vocation based on hearing about yours. St. Bernard of Clairvaux[93] is said to have brought thirty men with him to the monastery. Vocations beget vocations. Saints aren't like shooting stars as much as they are like constellations. It's time to let your light shine!

---

93   www.sbcwickford.org/history/bernard.html

Chapter Thirteen

The Stages of Religious Life

The main emotion I experienced when I finally entered the convent was joy, coupled with a sense of deep relief. In fact, it was like I was riding a great tidal wave of relief after the drama of my discernment finally came to an end. I was so overjoyed that I told the sisters on my first day I felt ready to lay prostrate before the altar and profess perpetual vows! There is, however, a big difference between *feeling* ready and *being* ready. The wisdom of Holy Mother Church requires a process of several stages to continue the discernment (for both the candidate and the community), to test the vocation, and to form[94] the woman into a religious sister—a daughter of the Church, a bride of Christ, and a servant of all, before making her perpetual profession. Every stage has its significance, and it is good for you to be able to look down the road a piece and see what's coming!

---

94 I use the word "form" rather than "train" because the concept of formation is much deeper. Religious formation includes a physical, moral, intellectual, and spiritual dimension. No part of the person is exempted.

Candidacy /Postulancy

After discernment comes the application process, and then, if accepted, entrance into the community. For many communities, entrance takes place in August or September. Communities have different names for the first stages of formation: candidacy, postulancy, or sometimes aspirancy. These are all essentially the same thing: the beginning of living in the convent with the sisters and learning their way of life. This is a time primarily for learning the externals—when to do what, and how to do it. Be assured that this is a joyous time! There is no laughter like that in the postulancy house! Since everything is new there are endless possibilities for mistakes, blunders, and mishaps. Not only does this keep you humble, but hopefully it keeps you smiling, too. At this early stage you want to take your vocation seriously, but do not take yourself too seriously! Let yourself make mistakes. Accept yourself with your imperfections and weaknesses, and be humble so as to learn. Rejoice in your vocation and in the Love that called you to the convent.

Investiture

After the pre-novitiate period, which could be anywhere from six months to two years, novitiate[95] follows. Many communities have a clothing ceremony or *investiture* which marks the beginning of the novitiate. In some communities, the investiture is accompanied by a ceremonial

---

95   "Novitiate" can refer both to the building where novices live and to the time period of this initial formation, similar to the word "college." The sister herself is called a novice.

cutting of the hair and the reception of a new religious name. The clothing is representative of laying aside the old self and putting on the new. The simple, common garb of a religious habit is a sign of your dying to the world and living a new life in Christ. The veil is a symbol of consecration—being chosen and set apart for the love and service of God and His beloved people.

I have been wearing a religious habit for nearly two decades now, and thus have managed to accumulate my fair share of interesting stories related to being so garbed. While friars may get mistaken for Jesus, or Moses, or even God the Father, we sisters have our own incidents of mistaken identity. Once, in the Midwest, I heard a small child exclaim to his mother as I passed their yard, "Look, mom! Just like the statue!" Sure enough, they had a lawn statue of the Blessed Virgin Mary. I was flattered. Once on a trip to a big city pool, I overheard one child say to another as the sisters arrived at the poolside, "The people from heaven are here!"

Every now and then we'll have an opportunity to see a deeper effect that the habit can have on others. When I was a new novice, I was on a field trip with some of our Bronx youth to a local amusement park. I was walking around the park with the five girls assigned to my care. As we walked along, we passed by two ladies resting on a bench. After we walked by, I heard one woman clearly exclaim to the other, "I've got to get back to Confession!" I was astonished. What a powerful tool for evangelization this habit was! I needn't say a word and conversions were just happening around me, or so it seemed to my novice-self.

This experience left a lasting impression on me. As new

and attractive as it all is—living in a convent, wearing a habit, receiving a new name—it's important not to get caught up in the externals. Novitiate is the time for *internal* work. Let the Lord into all the deepest places of your heart, mind, and soul. Formation is the work of the Holy Spirit and is meant to affect the whole person, from the inside out.

Novitiate

The period of novitiate is an intense time of formation intended to help you recognize your divine vocation and prepare you to live the vows. The novices all live together and are under the direction of a novice directress who meets with them regularly to teach, guide, encourage, and correct them. Currently it's popular to have a "life coach," and that's more-or-less what a novice directress is. Novices have classes in the evangelical counsels, the rule of life, theology, and philosophy, as well as training in topics related to the apostolate. This period must be at least one year and many communities have a two-year novitiate. While the pre-novitiate period is a chance to learn the routines and get the hang of things, as a novice you can focus more intentionally on your inner life—your spiritual and intellectual formation. There is more time for prayer and study, and if you dive into the fullness of this experience you are likely to grow in significant ways. You will get to know yourself better in the light of Christ, and to accept yourself with all your weaknesses and limitations as He accepts you.

The time of novitiate is necessarily intense. You may be wondering if there is ever an outlet; do sisters have an opportunity for fun? During recreation time, many sisters enjoy playing basketball, Frisbee, volleyball, tennis, soccer, and so forth. Some communities have a daily opportunity for sports. Some sisters also enjoy board games or puzzles. Most sisters like to read; some write poetry, sketch, paint, or write icons. Religious life provides many opportunities for singing and playing music together, and perhaps even composing and recording. Sisters in some communities learn handcrafts like knitting, sewing, and embroidery. Occasionally, on special occasions, sisters may watch a good film together.

It is important for you to enter fully into everything. Don't hold back and don't opt out! If it's time to meet with your novice directress, then be open and honest! If it's time to cut loose on the soccer field, then go for it—even if you don't feel like it! If it's time to fast, then fast. If it's time to feast, then feast! Entrust yourself to the process.

First Profession of Vows

At the conclusion of the novitiate, if you freely choose, you will profess public vows of poverty, chastity, and obedience, which are received by the Church. Typically there is a wedding-like feel to this joyous celebration. Most often, your family and perhaps others are welcome to celebrate this event with the community. I remember when I made first vows, after all the hubbub was over and all the guests were gone, I was alone in my cell and pondered what had happened to me. Everything felt more real; red seemed redder and the sky was bluer. I could only conclude that I was becoming more myself—that making vows had made me more *me*.

First Profession inaugurates a new stage of formation. You are now standing on the solid ground of consecration.

Your formation continues through your immediate superior, your spiritual director, prayer, study, and your work in the apostolate.[96]

Temporary vows are renewed over several years (up to nine if needed), allowing both your formation and your discernment process to continue.

Perpetual Profession

Making perpetual profession binds you to God forever. At this point you are freely vowing yourself to God in the service of others according to your community's constitutions. Many sisters, but not all, wear a ring to symbolize that their union with God is eternal. It is a solemn, yet joyous occasion. Formation continues for you even after perpetual vows. You must nourish your intimacy with Jesus in prayer and allow the Gospels to continue to form you. You will also continue to be formed through community life, study, and self-giving love in the apostolate.

There is so much that can be said about each of these stages! But suffice it for now simply to *know* the stages. As you continue your journey, the beauty and mystery of this life will unfold for you through the particular traditions of the community you are discerning with. Know that your vocation is a precious treasure, a pearl of great price. It is not too early to begin to humbly pray for the grace of perseverance.

---

96   *Directives on Formation in Religious Institutes* (The Congregation for Institutes of Consecrated Life and Societies of Apostolic Life)

Chapter Fourteen

Real Advice, Tried and True

"The way of the fool seems right in his own eyes, but he who listens to advice is wise."

~Proverbs 12:15

Sisters of several different religious communities from all over the country were asked what piece of advice, given to them in their own discernment process, really helped them in a significant way. Here is what they said.

Sr. Antonia

"In my discernment, when I got to a point of clarity but didn't know if I should enter right away or wait, someone gave me the advice to 'walk forward in faith.' I really did feel at peace about entering right away, but there seemed to be too many obstacles to do that. So I wrote down all the things that I felt were obstacles to entering right away and told the

Lord that if He opened the door and took care of each of these concerns, I would go through the door and enter. So that's what I did, fully expecting to hit a wall or a closed door at some point, but I never did."

Sr. Ann Kateri

"Perhaps one of the most helpful pieces of advice I received was the suggestion to make the spiritual exercises of St. Ignatius. I made a four-day retreat and a number of the meditations were extremely helpful for my discernment, especially meditating on Christ at the end of my life. In imagining what that moment would be like, I could see clearly the gift He was offering me in the call to be completely His, and that I would have to account for accepting or denying the gift. I could also see that I was free to choose to marry, but that grace and happiness would not always be there for me. It was the most honest time of soul-searching, and it led me to the clarity that Jesus had chosen me to be His, and this was at the heart of who I was."

Sr. Kelly Francis

"The greatest help to me was having a spiritual director. I was too close to everything to know what was really from God, and I needed guidance to know how to move forward."

Sr. Guadalupe

After coming to a clear realization that she did have a religious vocation, Sr. Guadalupe received this advice from her spiritual director: "It's time to make a visit." Sr. Guadalupe admitted that she delayed in arranging it, but her spiritual director persisted until finally she called the convent. Sr. Guadalupe visited the convent for a week, and in this visit everything crystallized for her. "I really enjoyed my time with the sisters. I loved the prayer life, and I thought the apostolate was a good fit for me." Suddenly she wanted to enter within the year. Visiting made all the difference.

Sr. Veronica

After writing a letter requesting to enter immediately (without finishing school), Sr. Veronica received a letter encouraging her to complete her degree and not to worry. The letter said, "If it's a real call from the Lord, it won't go away, it will only get stronger." These words "dispelled a hidden fear that somehow I would lose my call if I didn't act immediately, and brought a peace to my heart." A second helpful bit of advice, she said, "came from my mom who bought me a plaque for my college graduation with a very beautiful quote from Scripture: 'Trust the Lord with all your heart and lean not on your own understanding; in all your ways acknowledge Him and He shall direct your path' (Proverbs 3:5-6). This piece of Scripture served to support me through the years of waiting before my entrance to religious life. I memorized it and would pray it often."

Sr. Maria Teresa

"When I was discerning between the active and contemplative life, I felt willing to consider contemplative life, but I wasn't joyful about the prospect. I felt that it would be a great sacrifice, but I'd be willing to do it for the Lord. My whole perspective on discernment changed when my spiritual director told me that God wasn't calling me to do something I didn't desire, something that was only a sacrifice. He said God made me with the desires that I had and He wanted to fulfill them. He assured me that God was calling me to do something that would fulfill the deepest desires of my heart and bring me great joy. This realization gave me the freedom to pursue the active religious life wholeheartedly."

Sr. Chiara

"When I was on a 'come and see' I received the advice to 'stay close to the sacraments.' These words truly resounded in my heart. The more I stayed faithful to this advice, the harder it was to deny what was happening in my heart. The Lord was convicting me of my religious vocation, and I realized that it was time to start making important decisions, like breaking up with the young man I was dating, and beginning to visit religious communities. Staying close to the sacraments was the best advice I received because it allowed the Lord to have His way in my heart and mind."

Sr. Elizabeth

Sr. Elizabeth recounts a meeting with her spiritual director: "I was speaking with my director about a recent date. We spoke about the awkwardness, the anxiety, and the bland emotions. During the same meeting, I shared about a chance encounter with a religious sister on campus that left me bubbling with joy and enthusiasm, and the desire to simply be with her longer. The priest was able to help me see the difference between these two experiences. This was a key moment for me." Another aide to discernment, said Sr. Elizabeth, was a simple phrase: "'It doesn't matter if your initials come before or after your name.' The sentiment was that one vocation doesn't make you better than the other. It's about how you can love God the best."

Sr. Michael Marie

"A word of advice that helped me significantly in my discernment was, 'You have given the world so many chances, why don't you give God a chance?' As I reflect on this now, I realize that it is God Who in His mercy gave me chance after chance to find happiness and fulfillment in living this way of life with Him and for Him."

Sr. Mary Cecilia

"Mother Mary Francis[97] told me to 'drop my nets.' If God is calling, we don't tell him to wait a couple of years until I finish doing what I want to do. We get up and go like the apostles did. To me, the message was, 'Don't be afraid to set out into the deep and to give yourself to love. You will indeed find the hundredfold.'"

From these pearls of wisdom, you can see that there are

---

97   Mother Mary Francis, PCC was the abbess at Our Lady of Guadalupe Monastery in Roswell, NM until her death in 1996. She was a well-loved author of spiritual works including *A Right to be Merry* and *Strange Gods before Me.*

many who have navigated the choppy waters of discernment and have made it to the safe harbor of their true vocation. They have found the pearl of great price! I hope you find consolation from the knowledge that *you are not alone.*

Chapter Fifteen

Crossing the Threshold

"Behold, I have an open door before you which no one can close."
~Revelation 3:8

Where are you on the journey of discernment? To get where you are going, it helps to know where you stand right now. Which of these stages describes you?

1. **Not open.** "Truthfully, I'm not open to religious life as a possibility, but I do *desire* openness."

2. **Sincerely open.** "I'm open to God's call, but I have a lot of doubts and fears about religious life."

3. **Holy indifference.** "I would feel peaceful if God were to call me to marriage, religious life, or another vocation. I trust God's plan for me, whatever it is."

4. **Ready to discern.** "I'm ready to get serious and take the six-month discernment challenge."

5. **Taking action.** "I've reached a point in my discernment where intentional action is required, such as applying to a community."

If you can identify that you are at stage one, meaning you are *not open*, good for you for being honest with yourself. Honesty is so necessary for growing and going deeper in your relationship with God. Keep being real about how you feel, and what you think. If you continue to pray and allow God to become the center of your life, you will be led by Him. This is the whole point of the spiritual life: to be led. I do not mean that if you continue to pray and let the Lord lead, you will eventually enter into a serious discernment of religious life. Maybe you will and maybe you won't. Let the Lord lead; yours is to follow.

If you are at stage two, then your heart is opening spontaneously like a flower in sunlight, and the possibility of religious life holds a genuine attraction for you. This is the time to form your thinking, read good books, and to pray.

You are at stage three if you can say that you trust God with your life; no matter which way He leads, you are ready to follow. Now you can consider if God might be inviting you to take the "six-month discernment challenge." Stage four is making a commitment to the six-month challenge and all it entails. By the end of the six months, you should be at stage five, clear about the next good step and committed to taking it.

No matter which stage you are in, you are in a good place. Do not make the mistake of thinking life begins when you enter the convent, or it really begins when you receive the habit, or when you make vows. Jesus is on the path with you right now. Follow Him.

After my convoluted journey, I finally was able to make

a decisive step. Crossing the threshold of the convent as I arrived on September 19, 1998, was perhaps the most significant step of my life. The small brick convent dedicated to Our Lady of Guadalupe, situated on Bainbridge Avenue in the Bronx, New York, was the place chosen by the Lord for me. By this point I had no doubts. I was certain, and I was more deeply at peace than I had ever been. I would have taken my final vows right then, so deep was the assurance I felt that this was my vocation at last. What I had been resisting was in fact what I had been waiting for. How patient the Lord is! My journey of vocational discernment came to a beautiful end with my final profession of vows on September 13, 2004.

Lest you think this tale ends here with "happily ever after," the truth is that there have been many tests, trials, and crucibles along the way, and it would be wrong to delete these from memory. This is to be expected and no doubt there will be many more before the race is won. This is true for every disciple of Jesus Christ. Christianity without the cross is both meaningless and unreal. But there are also plenty of joys and blessings—too many to ever be counted, for all vocations are filled with light and shadows. It is the wellspring of peace beneath both the sorrows and joys that is the irreplaceable consequence of doing the will of God.

The goal of your discernment is to end in decision. You are not meant to remain in an indefinite state for the whole of your life. The tools of discernment learned before entering will be useful your whole life long as you continue to listen for the call of God in your life. He who called you to religious life is not going to stop calling after you enter. Entering is only the beginning. He means to fill your life with inspiration, and if you continue to follow Him, your life will be nothing other than an adventure of grace.

Acknowledgments

After our good God and dear Blessed Mother, my thanks begin with Sam Alzheimer, founder of Vianney Vocations. Having long desired a counterpart for *To Save a Thousand Souls*, Sam asked me if I would consider expanding the booklet *Is This a Call?* into a book. Without his passion to assist the discernment process for both men and women, this book would not exist. For his vision, encouragement, and professionalism, I am deeply grateful. Matt Yogus, Joshua Facemyer, and all at Vianney Vocations also have my heartfelt thanks.

Because my desire was to make this book truly universal and not merely promotional material for my own community, I consulted with many religious sisters from a variety of communities across the United States (plus one community in Belfast, Ireland). I am deeply grateful for every bit of input received; whether it made it into the final text or not, it was certainly a valuable part of the writing process.

If I fail here to list every person who assisted me, know that I have not failed to remember you all gratefully in my prayers. Special thanks to: Fr. Giuseppe Siniscalchi, CFR; Mother Joan Paul and the School Sisters of Christ the King, including very specially Sr. Mary Alma; Mother Juana Teresa and the Disciples of Our Lord Jesus Christ, especially Sr. Ana Chiara and Sr. Michael Marie; Mother Megan Mary and the Sisters of the Society of Our Lady of the Holy Trinity, especially Sr. Mary Emmanuel and Sr. Mary of Hope; Mother Angela and the Poor Clare Nuns Our Lady of Guadalupe Monastery in Roswell, NM, especially Sr. Claudette, Sr. Cecilia, and Sr. Clare; the Poor Clare Nuns of Alexandria, VA; Mother Josephine and the Sisters of Adoration and Reparation in Belfast, especially Sr. Máire of St. Joseph. A very special thanks also to Erin Welsh.

Additionally I am deeply grateful to: Sr. Maria Teresa Hellberg, CFR., Mercedes Augusta, Rachel Daly, Anne Marie Healy, Sr. Virginia Hebers, ASCJ, Mother Mary Clare Roufs, ACJ, Mother Joan Paul Tobin, CK, Fr. Bonaventure Rummell, CFR, and Sr. John Mary Flemming, OP for reading the manuscript and for your invaluable feedback which has made this a better book.

My own community was naturally a wellspring of stories and examples, as well as prayer and encouragement. A special thanks to each of the sisters whose names appear in these pages and to each and every sister for your loving intercession for me and for this book. Mother Lucille especially has my profound gratitude, not only for her ready "Yes" to this book project, but also for her "Yes" to my vocation from that first phone call to the present, and for her boundless encouragement, support, and love. Fr. Andrew Apostoli, CFR, too, has been a source of rock-like support in my vocation from day one.

Lastly, I remember my dear family, especially my mom and dad, Sharon and Michael Matthiass, who have given me the two greatest gifts: life and faith—the firm foundation for my vocation, for which there is no adequate thanks, only my unending love.

Appendix A: **Prayers**

Morning Offering

O Jesus, through the Immaculate Heart of Mary, I offer You my prayers, works, joys, and sufferings of this day for all the intentions of Your Sacred Heart, in union with the Holy Sacrifice of the Mass throughout the world, in thanksgiving for Your favors, in reparation for my sins, and in particular for the intentions of the Holy Father.

Consecration to the Blessed Virgin (According to St. Louis de Montfort)

I, [Name], a faithless sinner – renew and ratify today in thy hands, O Immaculate Mother, the vows of my Baptism; I renounce forever Satan, his pomps and works; and I give myself entirely to Jesus Christ, the Incarnate Wisdom, to carry my cross after Him all the days of my life, and to be more faithful to Him than I ever have before.

In the presence of all the heavenly court I choose thee this day for my Mother and Mistress. I deliver and consecrate to thee, as thy slave, my body and soul, my goods both interior and exterior, and even the value of all my good actions, past, present and future; leaving to thee entire and full right of disposing me, and all that belongs to me, without exception, according to thy good pleasure, for the greater glory of God, in time and eternity. Amen.

Consecration to the Blessed Virgin

O Mary, my Queen and my Mother, I give myself entirely to you, and to show my devotion to you, I consecrate to you this day my eyes, my ears, my mouth, my heart, my whole being without reserve. Wherefore, good Mother, as I am your own, keep me and guard me as your property and possession. Amen.

Short Consecration

I belong to you entirely
And all I possess is yours
I take you into everything
that is mine.
Give me your heart O Mary.

Prayer Before the Crucifix

Look down upon me good and gentle Jesus, while before Your face I humbly kneel, and with burning soul pray and beseech You to fix deep in my heart lively sentiments of faith, hope and charity, true contrition for my sins, and a firm purpose of amendment while I contemplate with deep love and tender pity Your five wounds, pondering over them within me, calling to mind the words which David Your prophet, said of You, my good Jesus: "They have pierced my hands and my feet; they have numbered all my bones."

Prayer by St. Francis of Assisi

High and Glorious God, enlighten the darkness of my heart, and give me true faith, certain hope, and perfect charity, sense and knowledge, Lord, that I may carry out Your holy and true command. Amen.

Radiating Christ

Dear Jesus, help me to spread Your fragrance everywhere I go. Flood my soul with Your Spirit and Life. Penetrate and possess my whole being, so utterly that my life may only be a radiance of Yours.

Shine through me and be so in me that every soul I come in contact with may feel Your presence in my soul. Let them look up and see no longer me but only Jesus!

Stay with me, and then I shall begin to shine as You shine; so to shine as to be a light to others; the light, O Jesus will be all from You, none of it will be mine; it will be You shining on others through me. Let me thus praise You in the way You love best, by shining on those around me. Let me proclaim You even without preaching, not by words but by example, by the catching force, the sympathetic influence of what I do, the evident fullness of the love my heart bears to You. Amen.

Suscipe Prayer of St. Ignatius

Take, O Lord, and receive my entire liberty, my memory, my understanding and my whole will. All that I am and all that I possess, Thou hast given me: I surrender it all to Thee to be disposed of according to Thy will. Give me only

Thy love and Thy grace; with these I will be rich enough and will desire nothing more. Amen.

Prayer for Generosity

Lord, teach me to be generous,
To serve You as You deserve,
To give and not count the cost,
To fight and not heed the wounds,
to toil and not to seek rest,
to labor and ask for no reward
save that of knowing I do Your will. Amen

Prayer of Abandonment

My Father,
I abandon myself into Your hands;
do with me what You will.
Whatever You may do, I thank You:
I am ready for all, I accept all.
Let only Your will be done in me,
and in all Your creatures.
I wish no more than this, O Lord.
Into Your hands I commend my soul;
I offer it to You
with all the love of my heart,
for I love You, Lord,
and so need to give myself,
to surrender myself into Your hands,
without reserve,
and with boundless confidence,
for You are my Father. Amen.

~Fr. Charles de Foucald

Appendix B: **Lectio Divina**

Lectio Divina is an ancient way of praying with the Scriptures. Some people find the Ignatian method difficult because of the emphasis on the imagination. Rumination on the Word is essential to this method but not vivid imagination.

Preparation: Select your scripture and a suitable place to pray. Recollect yourself and begin with an act humbling yourself before the Lord, such as a reverent sign of the cross.

Lectio: Attentive reading, aloud if possible. *What does the biblical text say in itself?*

Meditatio: Meditate and reflect using your intellect. *What does the biblical text say to me?*

Oratio: Speech, conversation, prayer. This is a time for dialogue with God about the word you are receiving in prayer. *What do I say to the Lord in response to His word?*

Contemplatio: Contemplation, or wordless prayer given by God. *What conversion of the mind, heart, and life is the Lord asking of me?*

Actio: Action. We do well to remember that the process of lectio divina is not concluded until we take an action which moves us to make a gift of our life to others in charity.[98]

---

98   *Adapted from Verbum Domini, 87.*

Appendix C: **Reading List**

In addition to the many Church documents cited in the footnotes, the following books are excellent means of furthering your personal understanding of the consecrated life, discernment, and the spiritual life.

FORMATION IN THE SPIRITUAL LIFE

A Heart To Know Thee: A Practical Summa of the Spiritual Life
E.J. Cuskelly, MSC

Called To Be Holy
Timothy Cardinal Dolan

He Leadeth Me
Fr. Walter Ciszek, SJ

I Believe in Love
Jean D'Elbee

Discerning the Will of God
Discernment of Spirits
The Examen Prayer
An Ignatian Introduction to Prayer and Meditation and Contemplation
Fr. Timothy Gallagher, OMV

Prayer Primer
Fire Within
Fr. Thomas Dubay, SM

FORMATION IN THE RELIGIOUS LIFE

When God Asks for an Undivided Heart
Fr. Andrew Apostoli, CFR

Poverty
Virginity
Obedience
Fr. Raniero Cantalamessa, OFM Cap.

And You are Christ's: The Charism of Virginity and the Celibate Life
Ecclesial Women: Towards a Theology of the Religious State
Fr. Thomas Dubay, S.M.

The Foundations of Religious Life: Revisiting the Vision
Council of Major Superiors of Women Religious

A Right to Be Merry
Chastity, Poverty and Obedience: Recovering the Vision for the Renewal
of Religious Life
Mother Mary Francis, P.C.C.

More Praise for *Discerning Religious Life*

"My first thought was, 'I wish I had read this when I was discerning my vocation!' Countless women will benefit from reading this book."

Sr. Megan Mary Thibodeau, SOLT
Superior, Society of Our Lady of the Most Holy Trinity

✠

"The tools offered in *Discerning Religious Life* will help you not only discover the will of God, but also give you the courage to respond with joy."

Bishop Andrew Cozzens
Archdiocese of Saint Paul and Minneapolis

✠

Discerning Religious Life provides concrete steps and authentic guidelines for discerning one's vocation. This much-needed book is a gift!

Mother Agnes Mary, S.V.
Chairperson of the CMSWR

✠

"With wit and wisdom, *Discerning Religious Life* brings insight to all who have wondered about a call. Readers will discover what Sr. Clare discovered: the Church wants to rejoice with you in your vocation, whatever that may be!"

Kelly Wahlquist
Founder of WINE: Women In the New Evangelization

✠

"I am so excited about this book! It's a wonderful resource that will inspire and empower women to listen attentively to God's will. We'll definitely be using it in our ministry."

Emily Savage, Founder of Fiat Ministries

✠

"A great resource not only for discerning young women, but also for bishops, priests, teachers, and lay faithful who seek to understand more deeply the gift of religious life and to accompany others as they embrace this call."

Mother Mary Clare, ACJ
Founder of the Handmaids of the Heart of Jesus